Younie, the Flea Market Doll

YOUNIE
THE FLEA MARKET DOLL

NOVEL

NORMAN BEAUPRÉ

Younie, The Flea Market Doll
Copyright ©2022 by Norman Beaupré

All rights reserved. No part of this book may be reproduced in any form or by any electronic or mechanical means, including information storage and retrieval systems, without permission in writing from the publisher and author, except by reviewers, who may quote brief
passages in a review.

This publication contains the opinions and ideas of its author. It is intended to provide helpful and informative material on the subjects addressed in the publication. The authors and publisher specically disclaim all responsibility for any liability, loss, or risk, personal or otherwise, which is incurred as a consequence, directly or indirectly, of the use and application of any of the contents of this book.

ISBN: 978-1-951901-89-9[Paperback Edition]
978-1-951901-90-5 [eBook Edition]

Dedicated to Victoria Perreault who loves anything that gives her pleasure like bagatelles and dolls… besides she speaks French. I truly believe that she will like and understand this story. Bonne lecture, Victoria

From the same author:

1. L'Enclume et le Couteau---Life and Work of Adelard Coté, Folk Artist, NMDC, Manchester, N.H., 1982, Reprint by Llumina Press, Coral Springs, Fl, 2002
2. Le Petit Mangeur de Fleurs, Ed. JCL, Chicoutimi, Quebec, 1999
3. Lumineau, Ed. JCL, Chicoutimi, Quebec, 2002
4. Marginal Enemies, Llumina Press, Coral Springs, Fl., 2004
5. Deux Femmes, Deux Rêves, Llumina Press, Coral Springs, Fl. 2005
6. La Souillonne, Monologue sur scène, Llumina Press, Coral Springs, Fl., 2006
7. Before All Dignity Is Lost, Llumina Press, Coral Springs, Fl., 2006
8. Trails Within, Meditation on the Walking Trails at the Ghost Ranch in Abiquiu, New Mexico, Llumina Press, Coral Springs, Fl., 2007
9. La Souillonne deusse, Llumina Press, Coral Springs, Fl., 2008
10. The Boy With the Blue Cap---Van Gogh in Arles, Llumina Press, Coral Springs, Fl., 2008
11. Voix Francophones de Chez Nous---contes et histoires par Normand Beaupré et autres, Llumina Press, Coral Springs, Fl., 2009
12. La Souillonne, Dramatic Monologue, translated from the French by the author, Llumina Press, Coral Springs, Fl., 2009
13. The Man With the Easel of Horn---the Life and Works of Émile Friant, Llumina Press, Coral Springs, Fl., 2010
14. The Little Eater of Bleeding Hearts, trans. from the French by the author, Llumina Press, Coral Springs,Fl., 2010
15. Simplicity in the Life of the Gospels---Spiritual Reflections, Llumina Press, Coral Springs, Fl., 2011
16. Madame Athanase T. Brindamour, raconteuse, histoires et folleries, Llumina Press, Coral Springs, Fl., 2012
17. Cajetan the Stargazer, Llumina Press, Coral Springs, Fl., 2012
18. L'Étranger Extraterrestre, Llumina Press, Plantation, Fl., 2013
19. Marie-Quat'e-Poches et Sarah Foshay, Llumina Press, Plantation, Fl., 2013
20. In Search of the Fallen Divina---Maria Callas, Llumina Press, Plantation, Fl., 2015

21.   Souvenances d'une Enfance Francophone Rêveuse, Llumina Press, Plantation, Fl., 2016
22.   The Day the Horses Went to the Fair---Animal Lover and Painter, Rosa Bonheur, LitFire Publishing, Atlanta, Ga, 2012
23.   Lucienne, la simple d'esprit, Lit Fire Publishing, Atlanta, Ga, 2017
24.   Of Boa Constrictors, Elephants and Imaginary Whales---Cautionary Tales, Stonewall Press, Bethsada, Md., 2018
25.   When the Flowers are Gone, Alpha Books United, Miami, Fl.,2020
26.   An Artist of Daring Creativity, Micheline Bousquet, Alpha Books United, Miami, Fl.,   2021
27.   Lucienne the Simple-Minded, Lucienne la simple d'esprit, trans. by the author, Alpha Books United, Miami, Fl.,2022
28.   La Souillonne et son cat'chisse en Images, Alpha Books United, Miami, Fl., 2022

INTRODUCTION

THIS IS A WORK OF CREATIVE FICTION BASED ON A DOLL that the author purchased in Paris at the flea market located at the Porte de Clignancourt, the last of the northern "doors" on the Metropolitain. I purchased the doll primarily because of a small yellowed sticker on its blouse that read , A ceux qui me possèdent j'apporte le bonheur/To those who possess me I bring happiness. I did not dare leave this doll behind, this doll of good fortune, as I called it. For me it had the sign or possibility of being a good omen. Who would leave the promise of happiness behind, I asked myself. The doll was a cheap plaything made of some kind of plastic with movable arms and legs, open and shut eyes, a round head, the semblance of curly hair, a pug nose and tiny puckered red lips. It was truly a cute doll, but I could tell it was old. It had a terribly faded wine-colored cap or kerchief on its head and it was tied in a knot at the top. It wore a black blouse with black pants all made of cheap cotton. It had black painted boots revealing toes that stuck out. Finally, the doll had a kind of faded gold-like scarf or ribbon around its neck.I first thought that probably the doll had been in a fire of some sort because its head had smoky black marks around its neck, ears, and under its eyes. It was a poor thing that had been lying around for years perhaps or possibly abandoned by someone, a poor child probably who now possessed a bigger or more expensive doll. Right from the start, I told myself, here is a doll that could tell us its story, where it came from, who had it, for how many years, and what places did it visit and adopted as a home, and more. As a writer, my vivid imagination could not help but to imagine all kinds of things that could relate to this plaything, this doll of good fortune, as I named it. I paid the lady at the table some centimes, I don't remember how many, and decided to take it with me. I really did not buy it for the doll itself but for the yellowed sticker on its blouse. I thought I had purchased an item that would inspire me to write a story about this flea market doll that some people might consider junk or undesired throw-away. I also bought a lovely yellow glass paperweight that I thought was artistically made. It's not very large with a rectangular shape. It features a raised leaf-shaped design on top of it and appears to be quite solid and well made in its esthetic sense. I still have it today. Eventually, I put the doll in a wooden box with a large label on top of it , "MADELEINES de COMMERCY" that I had gotten while in Paris. It reminded me of Marcel Proust's famous multi-parts novel, À la recherche du temps perdu, when he tells the reader of remembering eating a "madeleine" dipped in hot tea that kept spinning involuntary memories of the past in his head. That's how I see this doll, a catalyst that prompts me to write her story although my memories are quite voluntary.

    I trust you will enjoy the imaginings of my creative mind about a doll who happens to fall in the hands of a somewhat itinerant writer and traveler. I dare to begin not fully knowing where I'll be going with this doll. What am I doing with a doll anyway? Well, I'm not a sissy nor a doll-maker/collector. I'm a writer. That's all. A writer writes and spins tales. I must say that we hardly hear the term sissy anymore. Has it disappeared, I wonder. Just me and my crazy thoughts. I wonder why it seems to have disappeared. Growing up, I knew that the term "sissy" meant someone, a boy, who plays with "girl" toys and acts like a girl. It also meant a boy who threw a ball like a girl, walked like a girl and did things that girls usually did. If I look back on my past, I do remember playing with paper dolls(I had two sisters who played with them), although I did not play with real dolls. I did have a tendency to enjoy fine clothes and dainty things which was thought of as the domain of girls, but I played all the games outside with the neighborhood kids, boys and girls. Games like, "pass the ring", "colors", hide-and-go-seek, "norrite"(French for some kind of hide and seek), and other games. I did, at times, play "hop and skip" with chalk-made numbered squares that were on top of each other and that you had a piece of colored glass that you threw into one of the squares and hopped to go and fetch it, if I remember. I didn't like sports and I did not play sports, neither did my father. One thing that most boys played was baseball and I did not play baseball, and my throwing arm was bad. I threw like a girl, they said. When I happened to play in a game of baseball, because I was forced into it, I was inevitably placed in the right or left field where there was usually very little action. I never owned a baseball glove; most boys did. My father bought me an animal farm and a Lionel train set among other gifts for Christmas, but never a baseball glove. Although, I must say that I ran very well. Quite fast, as a matter of fact. So, I do not think that the term sissy can be applied to me even though I did purchase the flea market doll. But that was for literary purposes, I must say.

LA POUPÉE:
MON HISTOIRE/MY STORY

JE SUIS UNE POUPÉE. I am a doll. My name? I do not know how I got it but it's quite a strange one, Younie. Strange isn't it? Each little girl who owned me for a while gave me a name, sometimes a name that I did not like such as, Marie-Louise, Éléonore, Toutou, Francine, Loulou and that English name, Guenevere. I had one that I really liked but the poor little girl died of tuberculosis on me. Her name was Minouette and she had given me the name, Mistalou. I liked that. It reminded me of a former owner originally from Russia who grew up to be a ballet dancer. Her parents had moved to Paris from Russia which was under the dictatorship of Stalin. From what I could gather, Monsieur Stalin was a pretty terrible man, a horrible man who had many people killed for nothing. No reason at all except to get rid of some folks who displeased him in some way, I guess. Killing for nothing and worse the daring of killing. Wow! He must have been a man filled with hatred and bitterness. I don't know, but that's what I think. I'm just a cheap doll. I don't have much of a brain, if I have any. Do dolls have brains? I do not really know. They must have something in their heads. It cannot be entirely empty. I knew this little boy, I won't give you his name because that would not be kind of me, but he once took a large doll completely apart to find out what was insde the doll. Nothing. There was nothing inside except some rubber bands and some little springs, but here was a no-brain case. It was an empty and hollow head. I just could not imagine a doll with absolutely no brain. It had to have something, some kind of thinking part or mechanism just like the humans have. But, what

YOUNIE, THE FLEA MARKET DOLL

was it? It had to be imaginary, something that helped the doll, whatever doll, to think or at least remember certain things. After all, each doll has memories to recollect, some things of her past worthy of remembrance. Without that her life would be entirely empty, hollow and worthless. That's how I see things. Well, enough of that. I'm here to tell you my story. It's a long story with a lot of people, places, and events in it. One thing for sure, I do remember things. That's the product of my brain, whatever you may call it. I suppose a doll's brain is invisible, but it does exist, I tell you. If you do not like my story, you can put it down and walk away. However, I tell you that you will enjoy reading it. It's lively, exciting and at times, touching. You shall see. Stick with it. Enjoyment comes from reading without interruptions. So sit in a comfortable chair or lie down with your head on sweet fluffy pillows and read my story. Don't worry about sad or bothersome things such as doing the dishes, running errands or someone calling you names, even some bullying by someone you don't exactly like. Forget all of that. Enjoy the never-never land of joy-filled imaginings. Take my hand and let's go. Let us fly above the common and ordinary things in life. I tell you, the ordinary only flattens your judgement and eradicates your sense of flying over levels of dull and unimagined life. I make things extraordinary. The human brain and especially the heart love the extraordinary. It tells me that I am loved by so many since I am part of the extraordinary. I exist to open up what is beyond the ordinary and prove to people that dolls can speak and remember things in an extraordinary way. Believe me even if I am just a doll. A flea market doll on top of that. And my name is Younie, the flea market doll. The only doll that can tell you stories if you listen to me. It takes a special effort to do that, but it will work if you believe. Please believe in me, believe I can tell you my story and you will begin to hear sounds that will reach your ears and penetrate your heart. Believing is crucial and that's why I ask you to do so. Marvelous things can happen when you believe. I know, so believe in me as I believe in you since you are my reader. See, I know you believe already since your ears have perked up, your eyes are wide open and you are ready to listen to me. See, I can tell.

Let's see, my first recollection of an owner is of a little girl named Marianne LaChapelle. Her parents came from Lausanne originally. Marianne was a sweet and tiny little girl who had big blue eyes and a doll-like face. Yes, she had the complexion of a doll, pink and bright like painted dolls. Of course,

I wasn't one of these dolls since I was never painted like so many of them. All I had were painted lips, bright red. I suppose that the maker of dolls like me wanted to show that I had one thing that was bright and noticeable since everything else was dull and even black, except, of course, my face. And, yes, my sticker. That could impress people who thought of purchasing me. Imagine, happiness being part of a doll's purchase price. Anyway, it wasn't the little girl's parents who bought me but Marianne's aunt, her godmother Violette, who purchased me at a toy shop on the rue Chevreuse in Paris. I lay there on the shelf next to a little crib made of wicker and ribbons. Suddenly, someone held me in her hands and took me to the light of the large window where the sun's rays penetrated the panes of glass, and she took a good look at me and suddenly exclaimed, "Mais elle est donc coquette cette petite poupée, elle et son étiquette de bonheur"/ She is so cute this doll, she and her happiness sticker. "Mademoiselle, I want it for my godchild, my little Marianne. She will enjoy this cute doll and will treasure it since she has very few toys. Her parents are poor and cannot afford toys. There's just enough money for food and the necessary things like newspapers and sugar cubes. Poor Marianne plays with small bottles, a faded piece of red ribbon and an old rag doll that the neighbor has given her. Poor thing." So she paid eighty-five centimes for me, put me in her meshed bag and she walked out of the shop that had a large hand-painted sign that read Au Plaisir des Affamés du Bonheur. Imagine, to the pleasure of those famished for happiness. I went out of the gift shop lying down in the lady's large meshed bag thinking where am I going now.

    I was scared at first, scared of being displaced and sent away from the shop into a new home of poor people. Would they like me and would the little girl, Marianne, really like a cheap doll like me, I asked myself. So off we went, the lady with the meshed bag, her groceries and me tucked in next to the demi-baguette she had bought at the boulangerie. I didn't eat anything, so I only was able to see its crust and the good smell of fresh bread. Oh, it smelled so good. Yes, dolls like me can only imagine the taste of human food, but we can somehow smell through our fabricated pores. I love the smell of flowers too. When I see some and especially when someone who has just bought some gets close to me. I see the colors and the beautiful texture of the petals and I can smell their odors, They're all different, the lilacs have a distinct odor, the marigolds have a kind of pungent smell, the peonies have hardly any odor at all while the roses, oh, the lovely and oh, so beautiful lavish roses have a perfume I could die for. It enthralls everyone, even dolls like me. Moi, une poupée!

The lady brought me to a very simple house with bright red shutters and a front door painted yellow. Later on, I learned that it was painted yellow as a recollection of the painter Van Gogh's taste for yellow as a symbol of accueil, welcoming. Apparently he loved yellow, bright yellow as bright as the sun. Van Gogh, the crazy painter(I shouldn't say that. He was confused and his brain was affected a bit) but he loved the sun and its warmth. That's why he moved from Paris to Arles down south where he painted his much revered and beloved, La Nuit Étoilée/Starry Night. You see I learned a lot from the father of that poor family. He loved art and loved to talk about it. All the time. Did you know that artists create beauty just like God did. I'll talk about God later. That's another subject that I learned. Yes, the father loved beauty and talked about it to whoever wanted to listen to him. Sometimes, his wife got bored with it and walked away from her husband's talking about art and beauty. I guess she did not care for it. Some people don't. Too bad. I like beauty, beautiful flowers, beautiful things like morning sunrises and evening sunsets, and, of course, I adore beautiful words especially in poetry. That's another thing the father taught me, poetry, and he recited some poems when he felt lonely. His little daughter would just stand there and listen to him although I do not know if she understood everything he said. It didn't matter because she was learning something that was beautiful to the ears. Poetry does that. It enthralls you and casts its spell on the reader when the reader reads out loud pronouncing each word and making them ring out like soft and sweet sounding chimes. I know, since I do have some kind of hearing. Like that I can hear people talking, animals whispering in the dark, flies buzzing around, even ants softly speaking to one another. Did you know that ants could speak. Yes, they can. It's a very low and almost silent talk that only ants can understand and, of course, dolls like me. Sometimes you can hear sounds that are a mixture of of sounds. It can be very loud to listening ears and sometimes called cacaphony, a strange word. By the way, the father's name was Alphonse while the mother's name was Alphonsine sometimes called by her husband as Phonsine. That's how he called her. I know, I could hear him calling his wife when he needed her. Phonsine was a nice woman especially nice to her little daughter. She was a kind lady and a lovely woman. She had a nice face, a face that could allure anyone who looked at her. But she was always busy with things and the care of her little daughter. She loved her so much. Phonsine is the one who had convinced her husband to move away from the mountains of Switzerland to Paris. She could not stand the awful cold. Everywhere all the time, it was cold and it gave a terrible chill to the bones. She could not stand the everlasting chill that even affected the plants and the flowers. Of course, she knew that Switzerland was a nice country but the mountains were no place to settle there and raise a family. Mountains were nice for skiers and those who love the frost, the cold and the mountain air. But for those who love warmth, the warmth of the sun and the lovely warmth of people, mountains and their cold chill are not for them. So, they moved to Paris. Paris to Alphonsine was a city of brightness and warmth where she could enjoy so many things like flower markets, weekly marché aux puces/ flea markets where she could look around to see if she could afford certain things like pots and pans that she needed or lovely pillows that she would have loved to buy but could not.

You see they were poor. Alphonse was a cripple and he could not find a job. Phonsine tried to find some kind of a job but failed to do so. Besides, she had to take care of little Marianne. So the family was poor, poor in money, poor in resources and even poor in relatives except for old aunt Violette, who happened to be Marianne's godmother. That was one of the reasons that the family had moved to Paris, aunt Violette. She lived there in the quartier Clignancourt, where there was a giant flea market. Aunt Violette would go there almost every day except when she would spend her day at the chapelle des bonnes soeurs, as she called it, the rue du Bac chapel where the body of Saint Catherine Labouré could be found under the altar on the right. So many people went to that chapel, people from all over the world. They brought flowers with them and placed them on the steps of the main altar where one of the nuns picked them up to place them in vases for the adornment of the chapel. Violette loved the flea market, but she also loved the Paris shops where she could find almost anything if she happened to go to a shop where there were all kinds of bargains such as the little shop where she found me. Ah, yes, Violette the sweet little flower of a woman who was an eternal shopper, it seems. She had nothing else to do. Now and then she would visit the poor family and offer little Marianne some candy, just a simple thing like a little lollipop, un petit suçon. Marianne was simply delighted. She liked to show aunt Violette her little doll and aunt Violette would hold me in her wrinkled hands. Phonsine would tell Marianne that it was aunt Violette who had given her the doll and the little girl would go to the old aunt and give her a big hug. She learned to love the old aunt because although poor in things, the little girl was rich in love, in love-giving. Her parents had taught her the value of love. I, the doll, had learned it from their little girl who lavished me with her warm sense of love-giving. Besides her little bottles and her faded ribbon, the little girl had nothing else to play with. The mother, Phonsine, sometimes gave the little girl a slice of some apple she was peeling but that was to eat and not a plaything. The little girl's father was a wood carver and he used his pocketknife to carve things when he found a nice piece of wood somewhere. He liked to carve little birds, small horses and tiny grasshoppers that he offered to people who gave him some centimes for his work.

Alphonse so loved his daughter that he would spend most of his time thinking about what he could do to please her. He knew that she loved her little friend, Naomi, who lived not too far from them. They had moved from Romania to France not too long ago and the two girls had met at a recital given by the neighborhood association. The parents had brought the two girls to this event and both of the girls had soon gotten acquainted through sheer girlish warmth and pride, proud of themselves and proud of being there among people who showed their welcome in a bright and colorful way. They sang songs as these people welcomed each and every guest, grown-ups as well as children. The children all seemed to light up like glowing candles as soon as they started to hear the melodies blended with very warm smiles that turned the children's smiles into chuckles of innocent laughter. The ambiance exuded the glow of le bon accueil, a wholesome hospitality.

Naomi and Marianne got along very well so that the parents were amazed at the glow of contentment in the faces of each little girl. They did not need words to express their delight as well as their communication of feelings on that spot, but rather the mere gleam in each other's faces was enough to spark an interest in getting to know one another as new-found friends. Children are often like that. They either accept the warmth and delight of new-found friends or they simply refuse to accept the linkages between them, and so they shy away in order to escape what they do not like nor accept. I call it personality clash. I've often seen that among children that I met in the past. As a doll, I do not make friends with other dolls but I see my role as a human synthesizer. I synthesize, I meld doll wonders with human feelings and acceptance of the gift presented by someone who loves dolls and wants to share that love with either a relative or simply a lonely little girl like Marianne or even Naomi. Loneliness is so terrible at times, it can ruin one's gift of warmth and friendliness. It's like a turtle who hides it's head in its hard shell never to look at the world again. Loneliness is a breaker of jubilant feelings and can destroy how good one feels. I know. I'm only a little doll but I have feelings too and they can go crash when I get to feel the pangs of loneliness. You see, I was not made for loneliness; I was made to cheer up somebody, a little girl, even a lonely woman who loves dolls. Dolls are for everyone, even boys sometimes. It's too bad when boys are called sissies if they happen to play with one of us. I'd say like a Raggedy Andy, for example. By the way, Naomi called dolls papusar since she had retained some words in Romanian. Funny how traces of languages remain in some while others can hardly know one language. I can imitate quite a few. But, I'm only a doll. Some people are so good with languages. They pick it up right away. Brains, people, brains, it takes brains and I don't have one. Mmmmm...I guess I'm not brainy. Hahaha.

    I realize that playing with dolls makes one feel that she is playing with a semblance of a little human being. Dolls are often the imitation or replica of a human, I dare say. Some are realistically human while others are made up to be a combination of a particular little girl with the particularities of some other semblances. Take for instance the Cabbage Patch doll. They have some human qualities, the clothing particularity and what they call the cabbage patch idea, although I see nothing cabbage patch about them. Oh, there have been some really nice dolls in the past, some with porcelain faces, hands and legs with feet, some fabricated by an artist of good taste and skill who made dolls for all to see in an exquisite doll museum. I'm a very simple, dull, under-dressed and under-desirable little bumpkin of a doll, I would say. However, I like myself as is and I would not trade myself for another more costly, more delightful and rich-looking doll that Santa Claus brings to nice and not at all naughty little kids. I bring some delight to some poor kid while I realize that I'm part of the poor class in society, but, and I repeat, I BRING HAPPINESS TO THOSE WHO POSSESS ME. My sticker says so. Isn't that great? I think so.

YOUNIE, THE FLEA MARKET DOLL

Marianne's father asked me once if I knew all the dolls whose arms and legs as well as the eyes, if they moved. I told him, no. You see, Alphonse could talk to me. He had the rare privilege of talking to dolls like me since he could talk to anything that people called imaginary. He was an artist, a dreamer. So, I told him I didn't know each and every doll that still existed and who traveled around the world, met an awful lot of people and still liked dolls. All kinds of dolls. I told him that I, myself, did not play with dolls. I'm a doll so I like to play with humans. They're real, I mean really real. Then, he told me that I was real, not faked. Not a lie and not inauthentic. I am authentic. Authentically real. Who can say the opposite since no one truly knows me. I am who I am and no one, absolutely no one will ever really know me. Oh sure, they know my appearances, my frailties as a doll and my lack of beauty. But what is beauty, I ask them. No one, absolutely no one can describe nor define what beauty is. No one. Beauty is a quality, an ideal, a concept, something that cannot be defined. Not even the great teachers nor the sublime philosophers, sometimes the poet does. I wonder if God the Creator can do that. Define beauty. He sure creates it but define it. Mmmm. Can he use human words, I wonder. Even he or she cannot bring beauty up front and show its qualities and refined genuineness, I think. No, no one can absolutely reveal the mystery of beauty anymore than one can define love and pure soul. Oh sure, pure souls tend to mean a soul that is brimming with innocence. Innocence, the state of authentic being and true self, not corrupt, whatever that is. I am not a philosopher nor a theologian, but I learned a lot from some of them when I was displaced all over the world. Sure, I've traveled and I have learned from my experiences with humans. I just sit and listen like the great Buddha and the benevolent great spirit of native Americans, native Amazonians, native Africans, and who else I may claim to be native to any geographic location in this world. Native means first come, first to be endowed with the sacred mystery of pure thought, pure feeling, pure everything. I mean truly and deeply human. What does it take to be human? That's a good question. I don't know, I'm a doll. I wasn't created. I was made, fabricated. Someone said, one day while I was listening, that fabricated came from the latin homo faber, man the maker. There you have it. Man makes; he does not create. Oh, sure he can be creative but he does not create like God the Creator. Did God create me? No, he created me through the talent and capacities of a human whom he had created. I was born, if you want, through the intercessation of man the maker, or was it a woman? I don't know. I don't know everything, you know.

So you see my little friends, Marianne and Naomi were created but I was made. There you have it. I later learned that these two had talents, talents and abilities that would flourish some day and render them professionally known all over the world. But that takes tremendous effort and hard work on their part. Practice, practice, practice and more effort to make the talents come to full fruition. I'm not making this up. I learned it after years of listening attentively and openly. You see, one must be attentive to others who speak the truth about things and their life experiences. That's what it takes to discover authenticity. And, what is authenticity, you might ask. Authenticity is truth in reality. We get that by going to the very core of things. No covering up, no hypocrisy, no laundering, no lying, no pretense, no denials, and no mistrust of the truth. What is truth? That's a good and difficult question. It has come to a moment of a Socrates. I was told that he was a great Greek philosopher who said he knew nothing and simply asked questions to get at the truth. Did he ever get it? Well, they poisoned him before he could get to the full truth. That's what I was told. Some say he committed suicide, but I don't fully believe it. Who am I to judge people's actions and things anyway? I'm but a doll. Well, enough of this. Let's get back to my story, the story of a flea market doll.

Dolls are like the handprints of humanity. They corroborate the existence of real people who live and breathe on this earth of ours. Dolls remind one of the values associated with being alive and staying alive through the fullness of the power of the intellect and the heart. I may add, the soul too. If you believe in souls. Dolls don't have one. They were not created; they were made, remember? As the maker, man/woman make things and refine them whenever there's a need for it. Sometimes they lack the power of being creative. I had an artist friend who told me once that everyone, yes, everyone had the power to be creative, but so many ignored and even shunned it. Too bad, she said. Her name was Micheline. If you want to know more about that, read the biographer's book. Enough, enough of that. The core of my story has just begun and here is my story as a flea market doll. Not of great importance, but important to some people.

I'm the product of an Italian maker whom people called the "doll maker,"produttore di bambole. He not only made dolls like me but he loved making all kinds of things like stuffed animals and velvety pandas. Why pandas? I don't know, but he made them and some people bought them. He made good money by selling them. People love to have dolls, of course, but they also love having stuffed animals. I don't know why, but I would think it would be better to get the real thing, I mean the genuine animal like a cat or a tiger or even an owl.

You don't have to feed a stuffed animal and that's probably why people get them. A little boy once told me that, yes, you feed stuffed animals, you feed them love. Gosh, he was right.

Now, my story continues when I was sold at a small shop in Tuscany by an old lady named Octavia who had no children and operated a religious articles shop that also had other things like dolls and spinning tops made of wood. I love tops that boys wrap a strong string around the tops and then release them on the floor or on the sidewalk to let them spin round and round until they fall on their side, flat and exhausted of having lost their spinning energy. Then, they are ready to be picked up and put back into play. Boy, I so often wished I could own a top. But then I would not have been able to make it spin. You see, I don't have any real fingers, just make- believe ones.

Well, the shopkeeper gave the lady her change and me, the doll she had just bought. The lady was a visitor from France. She spoke French and Italian. She always spoke to me in French. That's how I learned French. "Ma belle petite poupée, she would say and keep on talking to me as if I could answer her back. Sometimes she would call me mia bambole. She probably thought she was till in Tuscany. It was all make-believe anyhow and we communicated somehow. The lady's name was Simone. One day, an old man came to visit her and he told her that the doll, that's me, was fine but had something missing. The lady asked him, what? He told her that I had no incentive for anyone to purchase me. She told him that she had no purpose to sell me. She wanted to keep me all to herself. "But, you could make a lot of money if the doll had something to interest people," he said.

---Interest people?

---Yes, interest people. Make them want to buy the doll at a very nice price. Then, you would make a nice profit.

---I don't want to make a profit. I want to keep her. I like her a lot. She brings me happiness.

---That's it. Put a sticker on her and let people know that the doll they buy will bring happiness to whoever possesses her.

--That's so strange, Edouard. People don't buy dolls that have stickers on them.

---They would if they see they could get something like a doll that guarantees them happiness. Besides, having a doll is having some happy moments. But, having one that offers happiness is a token of good fortune. I tell you Simone, things will change for you if you start selling dolls with happiness stickers.

---Where would I get the dolls?

---I can get some for you. We can create a specialty shop, une boutique de poupées heureuses.

And they both laughed. So Simone and Edouard got a start on a profitable venture with "happiness dolls." I was the very first one, you see. I wasn't sure if I would like having a sticker on my black blouse but there was nothing I could do about it except to stay there lying on the shelf. What was that going to look like, I asked myself. A sticker? People like stickers. They give them a kind of notification about something, but a sticker about happiness? I couldn't get that out of my mind. I was a happiness doll. That's what Edouard called me. I learned to say, "J'apporte le bonheur/I bring happiness. I certainly hoped so. I would sure try. What is happiness anyway? It's a state of being that satisfies the hunger for goodness and smiling faces. Happiness brings delight and satisfaction when one has done something pleasant and satisfying to oneself and to others. I found out that happiness can be contagious. It rubs off you and rubs in another. How does it do it? Well, it does it by a great big smile, not by an awful frown. Frowns are the signs of unhappiness and dissatisfaction. So people have to learn to change the downside ends of a frown into upside ends of a smile. It's easy. Some people have downside ends on their lips all the time. It's terrible. It's down sad. I feel sorry for them. They're always frowning and spreading gloom around them. Someone should write a song about that. "Turn it up, turn it up and give me a smile," I would suggest as part of the lyrics.

Well, someone did come into the shop of happiness dolls and that someone purchased me. Why? I don't really know since I was not beautiful, lying down with my eyes closed with black clothes on. Cheap black clothes too. I did not look pretty enough to buy, I thought. But, that someone whose name was Georgette did buy me just because, she said, I looked adorable in my simple black blouse with a happiness sticker on it. I did not think so but she did. I opened my eyes because I wanted to take a good look at her. She was pretty with auburn hair and blue eyes. I liked her. Her first words to me were, "Viens, ma poupée, je t'apporte chez moi pour donner un peu de bonheur à ma mère"/I'm bringing you home so that you can bring a little bit of happiness to my mother. I did not know then but her mother was sick with a debilitating illness called heart failure. The doctors could not do anything about it. Everyone except her daughter had given up on her. It's so sad when people give up on you. It makes you feel unwanted and cast aside like a used plaything, like a worn out and tattered Raggedy Ann. It is indeed sad when one sees a Raggedy Ann practically fall in pieces. Nobody, but nobody pays any attention to the poor things. All they want to do with them is throw them in the dump. I met one such doll once. She looked terrible practically falling apart with her red hair all frazzled and unkempt. She certainly was not going to bring happiness to anyone. She was a mess with a messy future. I don't know if someone picked her up or not . All I know is that she disappeared one day and I never saw her again. I shed a few tears. It was so sad to see a doll in such a predicament. Dolls should never be mistreated, especially thrown away for good. I hope it never happens to me.

Georgette's mother was in a sad shape. She could hardly walk and she moaned all the time. She said that she was in pain most of the time. Her daughter tried to relieve her pain and bring a little sunshine into her life but it seemed that nothing worked. There was no happiness in both the mother's and daughter's sad existence. Only pain and suffering. So when she brought me home, she gave me to her mother telling her "Maman, je vous apporte bonheur"/I bring you happiness. The mother smiled but then her smile turned to sadness. She told her daughter that she did not need a doll to bring her happiness. She told her daughter that dolls were for little girls and how dare she give her own mother such a cheap doll that looked like a flea market deal. The daughter answered her by saying that the doll did not come from a flea market but from a lovely shop where they sold quality items. The daughter thought that the little doll would cheer her up and that she could give me a name if she wanted to. The mother's name was, Ophélie.

Well, Ophélie did not want to give a name to a doll, she said. She felt insulted that her daughter would do such a thing. Bring home a doll for a mother who was eighty-five and in constant pain. She did not need a joke, she told her and she certainly did not want to believe that a doll would bring her happiness. She was angry at her daughter, Georgette. The daughter could not help but shed a few tears when Ophélie was accusing her of making fun of her. Afterwards, the mother repented of having talked like that and making her daughter cry. So, she took the doll and put her, that's me, in her knitting basket where I lay there for quite some time, four days, if I remember. I didn't know if she was ever going to take me out or not. However, she did and she started examining me from head to my painted black boots. She kept turning me around and looking if she could find something strange about me. No, nothing strange but the sticker intrigued her. She almost tried to take it off until her daughter saw her doing it and told her bluntly not to try taking the sticker out. It belonged there and should stay there. It was, after all, part of the purchase. It was intrinsinctly part of the doll, she told her mother. Hey, that was me, and it was part of me the poor doll with black clothes on with eyes that open and shut and with arms and legs that moved. I was quite the doll. In a way I was part doll part human, so I thought.

People asked me where I had gotten all my long words and deep thoughts on certain matters such as philosophy and religious subjects as well as literature. Well, I told them that I had gotten it from listening to people in the know and I was so fascinated by everything they talked about that I decided to pay really close attention to it. That's how you learn. I knew that; everyone knows that, don't they? I did learn later on that not everyone is captivated by knowledge and truth and interesting lives and events. They simply shrug it off

YOUNIE, THE FLEA MARKET DOLL

like shooing off a fly. How can I discuss anything serious if I don't have the knowledge to do so and the matter to deal with. I did not go to school but I learned to learn. Every single day I learned something enough to reduce my sense of ignorance. It's terrible being ignorant. Ignorant of things, ignorant of history, ignorant of ideas that have been passed down from generation to generation of people gathering together the strains of good existence that ultimately form the core of what is considered human. Being human means to be endowed with a voice, a brain, a heart and a soul and transforming them into learning vessels. Human beings are not created to remain ignorant the rest of their lives. I was told once by this old native American sorcerer when I was brought to North America for a visit that intelligence is a God-given thing and the Great Manitou expects his creation to be an open vessel to all learning be it in nature, with animals, with other forms of life, with all creatures and especially with other human beings be they red-skin, white-skin, black-skin or any other color. Color in human beings does not matter. It's just skin color. The heart and soul do not recognize color So, if I do not look at color only in human beings, I must look for the interchange of feelings and ideas that are so often exchanged. Some people prefer violence instead of peaceful gestures. Peace comes from the heart not the face color nor the swipe of each hand that seeks violence and revenge. I do not seek anything except doll peace, a peace that renders one completely satisfied with one's feelimgs and one's ideas accumulated in the receptacle of the brain. The brain is a receptacle not a hollow indifferent machine that seeks so-called money and reputation. Pride and greed are the motivators here. I won't want any of that. No, 'mam, All I want is a good home, good people, good children and peace. Of course, there are peace-loving people and people who do not know what peace is nor do they seek it. You don't seek something you don't know anything about. So, you live in utter ignorance of the things you should know or, at least, you should pursue the best you can. The pursuit of truth and knowledge is soul searching, I heard someone say that one time. I never forgot it. My brain may not exist but my memory is certainly not dead. I always dread losing my memory like so many people with dementia do. God bless them. They have become almost like vegetables with their heads buried in the soil waiting to be harvested. That's alright for them but not for us, humans or doll-like beings with human features such as me. That's what I consider myself, a doll with human features and hunan possibilities. Nothing else. All I can say is what I have lived for, kindness, knowledge, mercy with others, words put into songs and words as poetry, and especially tenderness towards yourself and others. You must treat yourself tenderly and with understanding of virtues and faults that are human and portray the very existence of a genuine human being in motion, the motion of existing and forging ahead. I love people who forge ahead and do not remain passive all the time. You know, that I-do-not-care-look and feeling. I told myself a long time ago, do not stand still and remain passive, be active and live. I had a guardian once who kept saying passivity is for the deadheads, those who are forever dead in the head and the heart that does not tolerate a brain that is dead for that's when a heart attack occurs, a stroke or any other shattering illness. Sickness often comes from shunted feelings, feelings that are rebuffed and never let out. We need air, the heart needs air, the brain needs air, the whole of any human being needs air and the loosening of the tightness of the heart. Let everything loose, told me some stranger one night as I was looking outside my open window by the silence of the soft glow of moonlight. The stranger was just walking alone and mumbling to himself about people who never enjoy moonbeams and crickets chirping in the night. Nighttime is such a delightful time of day. It's when I can feel the calm and the quietude of the heartbeat throbbing with delight. Oh, I do feel it now. Right now. I do have a heart, you know. You may not be able to see it or prove it, but I do have one. I feel. Je le sens. Je sens son battement qui est invisible mais réel/I feel its beating which is invisible but real.

Anyway, Georgette's mother got tired of me. I think she was ashamed of having a doll at her age and that people would laugh at her. So, she kept pressing her daughter to get rid of me. Her daughter told her she could not return her purchase since the shopkeeper would not accept it. Ophéline kept insisting and insisting until her daughter decided to return me to the shop of Au Plaisir des Affamés du Bonheur. I smiled when I was told that meant "To the pleasure of those famished for happiness."

The shopkeeper was not too pleased to accept a doll that had been sold since she told Georgette that the shop had no refund, no return policy.
--How can I accept a doll that's been gone from my shop quite a while?
---But my mother does not want it inside the house.

YOUNIE, THE FLEA MARKET DOLL

---Sorry, but I cannot take it back nor give you back the money you paid.   A sale is a sale. Final.

---Just give me part of the money. Just half or else I'll have to throw the doll away. My mother and I don't want it. Final.

---But Madame, you cannot force me to do what you insist I do, return an unwanted doll.

It is then that I learned that I had become unwanted. What a terrible thing to hear from people. Unwanted.

---I do insist and I will complain to people about you and your shop and you will lose customers.It will hurt your business.

She then pushed me, the doll, right in her face. I felt so bad.

---Here take it. I do not want it.

Here we go again, wanted and unwanted, I said to myself. It's so sad not to be wanted.

So the shopkeeper took me back, examining me before doing so and then put me back on the shelf.

She then gave Georgette some centimes. I do no know how many. I simply felt abandoned before I even had the chance to bring a little happiness to the old mother. Anyhow, she did not want me and she did not want happiness. I only bring happiness when the one who possesses me wants happiness. That's one thing I know for sure. I'm not dumb, you know.

That's when Violette bought me for little Marianne. The shopkeeper was delighted to sell me again without any regrets nor complaints on Violette's part. The shopkeeper did tell Violette that there was no return and no refund. Violette answered her that she did not plan to return the doll. "Non, Madame. I do not buy nor do I return used dolls." The shopkeeper said nothing. She simply took Violette's money and smiled. Quatre-vingt-onze centimes.

Violette rushed home, took her coat off and went to get a box from a closet and set it down on the kitchen table. She then opened the box, took a bright pink ribbon and tied it in a big bow. She then took the package she got from the shop(that was me in the package)and she tied he ribbon and bow around it. She got dressed again and went to her niece's and nephew's house where Marianne lived. She was all excited. She could hardly wait to see the joy in Marianne's eyes when she gave her the surprise package. Alphonse and Alphonsine did not expect Violette's visit. They were a bit surprised and somewhat nervous seeing their aunt there at their door so early in the week. I just stood there lying down in the package utterly still. I didn't know what to expect until I was placed in Marianne's small hands. She very quickly opened the package and saw me for the first time. She cried out, "Oh, maman, qu'elle est belle! C'est un beau cadeau!"/It's lovely, it's such a nice gift. Marianne had never gotten a doll before. Her parents could not afford it, you see. I was delighted. Someone wanted me. It's so nice to be wanted and loved.

--What do you say to aunt Violette? said the papa.

---Merci.

---Now go and give her a big kiss, dear sweet one.

Marianne ran over and kissed Violette on the cheek. Violette was all smiles. She had a tear in both eyes.

---Thank you so much aunt. Marianne will be very happy with this little doll. She's so beautiful with her blinking eyes and her small arms that move. Wait, I see a small sticker on her blouse, said Phonsine.

----Yes, it is a sticker. Read it, my dear, said Violette.

Of course, I knew what was on it. It was right on my blouse and some people had already taken a look at it.

---A ceux qui me possèdent j'apporte le bonheur, read the mother.

----Yes, exactly, replied the old aunt.

----Why how good of you to bring us happiness, said Alphonse. This house needs it.

----Papa, can I see it?

----See what my sweet?

---Happiness, papa.

---Why you have it right in your hands. It comes with your doll.

---Oh, papa, it's such a nice doll, une poupée à moi, ma poupée, my doll.

And so I realized then that I was truly wanted. I belonged to someone. I was glad.

Marianne took very good care of me. She pretended washing me every morning just to keep me clean. I didn't need to be washed but it was good that the little girl respected cleanliness. Clean is good.

Marianne grew up tall and slender. People remarked that she had grown to be a very pretty girl. She attracted boys who tried to become very close to her enough to be called boyfriends, but she refused every advance. She wanted to be left alone. She had no plans for being attached to anyone not even a boy she liked. Marianne wanted to finish her education and then travel to Brazil where one of her teachers had settled. That teacher was a member of a religious community called the Sisters of the Good Shepherd. They had a mission in Natal that they named Bom Pastor. Their work dealt with street urchins whose parents were under the influence of alcohol and did not provide a home for their children. The nuns also took in girls who prowled the streets for food and money and became innocent girls of the night or prostitutes. Some were as young as fourteen.

After high school, Marianne sought contact with Sister Marie-Viola, her former teacher and tried to get permission to go to Bom Pastor and volunteer her services. At first, she was denied permission to go to the mission compound because the nuns thought she was too young to do such social services with the excluded ones from society. That's what they were called, the poor helpless ones the nuns cared for. Marianne insisted so hard and so often that finally she was given provisionary permission to go to Bom Pastor.

Marianne did all the paperwork necessary from passport to health records and was prepared to leave when she encountered a hitch in her plans. She was told that community's mother house would not sign the document due to inconsistencies with the community's policies. It was ruled that such a visit would create difficulties and the older nuns in the chapter voted against such probable inconsistencies that were seen as unacceptable. Sister Marie-Viola appealed the case but it was not until personal contact was made to the Mother General that permission was finally granted. For you see, Marie-Viola and Mother General, known as Marie-Léonard were students together in the novitiate and became good friends although the rules opposed any kind of friendship in community life. However, friendships are natural and they form rules or no rules. They are kept hidden in the heart.

Once in Brazil, Marianne studied the language of Brazil which is Portuguese. She found it hard at first but through study and perseverance and especially cultural immersion, Marianne was able to become quite fluent in the language. She even tried to teach me a few words but they became tongue twisters for me, a poor little doll. Yes, Marianne had taken me with her to Brazil. It was my second trip in a jet plane. I was packed with her clothes so it was a soft ride for me.

Marianne was introduced to the children at Bom Pastor as well as some of the girls who were called street-walkers by others, not the nuns. Marianne called them loners or poor things. She felt sorry for them these prostitutes of the streets, alone and looking for food and money. Once their relationships with the men ended, they were abandoned and left to fend for themselves. They suffered cruelty and loneliness. Finding out they had become pregnant, the only recourse for them was some kind of social aid that was not always available except at Bom pastor which was known to be welcoming and asked no questions. The problem was that once the baby was delivered and given away to some eligible parent, the girl returned to the streets and plied her trade as street walker. The nuns would give her some lemons to sell and make some money but the money was soon gone and the girl would return to the convent refuge, pregnant and poor. I learned all of that from some of the girls who came to Marianne and spoke to her quietly and secretly.

There was one pregnant girl who was fourteen and a half named Maria -Imelda who came almost every evening to sit with us next to the garden. The lovely garden was a favorite place of Marianne. Mine too, for you see she always brought me with her. She was ever the young girl at heart with her poupée de bonheur. Maria-Imelda asked her about me and Marianne told her everything, that I was an extraordinary doll with a sticker on her blouse that read "I bring happiness to anyone who possesses me" The poor thing asked Marianne if she could hold me in her hands. Of course, Marianne did not refuse. The poor Brazilian girl was gentle and came to tears just holding me. Marianne asked her,

YOUNIE, THE FLEA MARKET DOLL

---Why are you crying?
---Because I never had a doll. Never. My parents were poor and all I saw of them was when they came home to give we the children some bread and jam, then they would go back to their drunken binges. We children were left alone and hungry for days.

Poor, poor Maria-Imelda, I felt so sad for her. Some of her tears fell on my blouse, even on my sticker of happiness. I certainly did not bring happiness to her. But, after all, she did not possess me.

Maria-Imelda lost her baby and worse than that she died three days after delivery. She died of an serious infection. A group of us brought the body to the nearby cemetery and a few prayers were said. The parents refused to come to the burial. I was shocked that parents like them did not consider their children with love and compassion. As we went out the cemetery Marianne picked up a doll with pins stuck in it, right on the ground. Marianne did not know if she should keep it or not. Sister Marie-Viola explained to Marianne that most probably the doll was a voodoo doll left there after some kind of ceremony where the doll is burned and left on the ground. Everyone told Marianne to dispose of the voodoo doll since it meant a bad omen and ill fortune for anyone who held on to it. It was not like me. It certainly did not bring happiness. Marianne kept it until the night before her departure for home in France. One of the other volunteers told Marianne that she had better get rid of the voodoo doll or something bad would happen and the plane would have a terrible accident. She so frightened Marianne that my good friend had me in one hand and the voodoo doll in the other when she decided to dispose of the dangerous one. No voodoo doll to bring home, just me the happiness doll. I was so pleased with her decision for I was scared also. I did not wish any doll a bad fate but voodoo dolls are different and they bring unhappiness. I know. I found that out in a dream. Yes, dolls do dream or I should say that it was a nightmare. Nightmares are never good. They bring bad news and scare the daylights out of people and, I might add, dolls. I love dreams for they bring me good thoughts and promises for the future, but nightmares, no, no, no, I do not like them. They frighten me and leave me to wake up shivering and breathing hard. Besides, I was waiting for a dream when it would be announced where I would be going and who was going to get me. You see, Marianne was going to college and she was going to give me to someone else. Someone she had met and had shown great interest in me la poupée de bonheur. Her name was Rose-Hélène.

I found myself in Québec, a large city in eastern Canada where people speak French. You see, Marianne had met Rose-Hélène at a Francophone conference in Paris where several invited guests came from Francophone countries or areas that speak French. I learned that Francophone meant just that French-speaking. Rose-Hélène knew that I had learned French with Marianne and that I understood it well enough, so she tried to teach me all about Québec and its history and culture. She was a good teacher and I learned a lot from her. She was a good cook too and she was very interested in food and cooking. I don't eat human food, not even doll food(there isn't any anyway) but I'm always interested in what humans eat. I know there are dolls with baby bottles whose small nipples can be inserted in the doll's mouth, but that's only pretend. I don't have one and I don't want one either. I'm a 100% doll. Don't try to change me.

What Rose-Hélène tried to tell me about Québec food was the pork pies called tourtières, that people ate specially at Christmas. Then there was the cretons, the pork spread, the crêpes avec du sirop d'érable/ with maple syrup, rôti de lard avec des patates jaunes/roast pork with yellowed potatoes and several other dishes. I cannot give you all of them. Those people eat a lot of food. They sure love food especially homemade food. Then there was the songs they would sing at veillées, the evening parties when family and friends get together play the violin, the accordion,the spoons(I never saw or heard of that before), and there was always someone who stood up and started to sing. There were all kinds of songs, hand-me down songs, they said, like the chansons à répondre, those are songs with repetitions from the people repeating what was just sung. Then, of course, there was dancing like the quadrille and some kind of square dance except they did not call it that. Of course, there was storytelling. Some old timer would tell the story of la Corriveau, apparently a woman who had killed her husband. I did not like that story. And, there was the story of Maria Chapdeleine and her lover, François, who dies in the wilderness during a snowstorm. I found that very touching and sad. Poor Maria Chapdeleine. And, there was the story in history books about Samuel de Champlain who came from France and founded the city of Quebec. At first, he and his men went to some colony where the Indians lived and they tried to live there themselves but found it much too cold in the winter months. They went back to France only to return to the Quebec settlement. Champlain even went to a river further south where the Almouchiquois Indians lived. He learned a lot about these natives and even wrote a book about his discoveries. In a chapter about these Indians he describes how they looked and lived. I heard many comments about that book. I don't read, so I didn't even look at the book. One of the history buffs who was at the soirée, I went to with Rose-Hélène and her family tried to interest Rose-Hélène into borrowing the book but she said she didn't have time to read. She had a job and she worked up to twelve hours a day as a nurse at the local hospital. I stayed in her room lying down on her bed all day long. It got to be boring. The mother would, at times, come in and straighten the room, fluff up the pillows and put me on the seat of a chair face down. I could not move nor could I breathe. I wanted to tell her to turn me around on my back. People don't realize that even dolls like me have to breathe.

When Rose-Hélène came home in the evening, she would pick me up and sing me a song that she had learned as a child from her grandmother Bellefeuille. "Dodo enfant-do, enfant dormira bientôt, make dodo, the child will sleep soon, she sang. But, I had slept all day, I didn't want to go to sleep, not now. She would look at me and realize what I wanted. I wanted a story, a nice story about dolls and animals. So, she would think for a moment and come up with one of her favorites, "La Petite fille aux allumettes"/the Little Match Girl. It was such a delightful but sad story. I truly liked it. I was scared of matches. I didn't like the fact that they could start a fire, and I hated fires. I never want to be in one. It's dangerous and downright frightening, but I like the little Match Girl story. Everyone knows the story so I don't have to tell it to you. It's about a young girl who is poor and alone and cold out in the streets on night trying to sell matches but no one buys any. She lights one match at a time to keep warm and has visions of her grandmother, the only person who ever loved her. Well, I don't have to tell you the rest. It's a fairy tale. I love fairy tales. They put me to sleep or rather they help me to fall into dreamland. Isn't there a better place than the land of dreams? I doubt it. You see even dolls like me love dreaming about someone or something. I go floating in la-la-land and dream. I dream of the happiness that I'll bring to the one who is going to possess me. I mean possess me for good, not just borrow me for some time or other. Possession is for real, for good and it means someone truly and deeply wanting me. Ah, to be wanted is happiness. That's what I think Rose-Hélène loved ice cream and every Saturday she would go to the ice cream parlor to get a cone of chocolate ice cream. She would pretend giving me a lick. I only wished that I could taste the lick but I couldn't. One Saturday morning, while Rose-Hélène was sitting in the ice cream parlor waiting to be served, a young boy practically in rags came into the parlor looking around and then begging anyone for a few coins. People tried to shoo him away. They did not like dirty little faces and boys dressed in rags, they said. The owner told the boy to get out and that he was not welcomed there. I remembered that meant not wanted. That's sad. You know what I mean. Rose-Hélène got up and took the boy's hand and brought him to our table. He asked what was the doll doing there. That was me. She told him that I was her friend and that I came from far away. He tried to pick me up but she told him not to. He began to have tears in his sad eyes. He put me back on the table. I felt sad for him. I so wanted to be held in his hands. He wanted me and I wanted him. I felt sorry for the little boy. I feel sorry for anyone who wants someone or something that she cannot have. It was then that Rose-Hélène told the little boy that she did not have any money to give him, only the money for her ice cream but that she would share the ice cream with him. There was a huge smile on his face. I smiled too. inside, of course, but I smiled with doll joy. Dolls can feel joy, you know. So, my friend went to get her ice cream cone and came back to our table. I could see that she saw in the boy's eyes the delight of an ice cream cone. His eyes became bright, lit with the fire of intense desire. Rose-Hélène could not help herself, she offered the entire chocolate ice cream(chocolate was her favorite) cone to the boy. At first, he was so surprised that he didn't want to take it for fear of feeling regret and possibly shame. My friend insisted telling him that she could get another cone another day. We both felt happy with delight when the boy in tatters took the cone and started licking with delight. His face was like sunshine full of light and happiness. Indeed, I was bringing happiness not only to my friend but to this young boy. He never got to have an ice cream cone, he told Rose-Hélène. Never. My friend started to have tears in her eyes and I felt the joy and sadness that she herself felt. It was such a happy moment that Saturday morning. I'm telling you, it doesn't take much to have happiness come into your life. You must wish for it as well as you have to earn it with good thoughts and especially with the intent of giving. Giving is a token of love, my friends. Not just giving things but feelings that you have. Humans often lack the real feeling of giving. If the feeling is real then it's a feeling that comes from the heart not the brain. The heart has a way of giving that the brain doesn't have. Rose-Hélène reminded me of Pascal's saying, "Le coeur a ses raisons que le raison ne connaît pas. So true, I told her. The heart does have a special place where feelings are lodged and the rational powers cannot fully understand or even describe. I'm not sentimental about this. It's just what it is. Ideas are ideas and feelings are feelings. Some people try to rationalize feelings all the time but it doesn't work. So give, give whenever you can for by giving you get a taste of happiness through feelings. Just like licking an ice cream cone.

  There came a time for me to get moving again. Rose-Hélène cried when she had to give me up. She had to because Marianne had made her promise to give me to another friend of hers who lived in Maine. Here we go again, I said to myself. But, why Maine. Where's Maine anyway? I found out it was south of Quebec along the Atlantic coast. So, I would get to see the ocean. Wow! I always wanted to see an ocean. While in Brazil I could have seen the Atlantic ocean but no one took me to see it. They kept me off the coast inside of Natal. I had heard them speak of the warm waters of the ocean and the many outings people took to spend an entire day at some beaches, but I never had the chance. All of my movements were lead by human decisions. Sometimes it's hard being a doll because you cannot choose what you want and where you are going to go. A doll like me has to follow all the time, just like kids who have to rely on the grown-ups' decisions and whims. I don't care since I'm a doll and I have no reason to complain. But sometimes I wish I did have the power of complaining because I would tell some people how I did not like what they were doing and why they were hurting others they did not like or respect. I can tell when people behave like wild animals. Why even wild animals behave better than them most of the time. Some people don't even like dolls and they even mistreat them just like they mistreat other people. I have seen some mistreat dolls by hacking them, cutting their heads off, pulling their arms and legs, stomping on them and then throwing them in the garbage cans. Just because they're angry at someone or something. Anger doesn't solve anything except to reveal how stupid a person can be. If a person has a brain he should be able to control his anger. Otherwise, he's unhappy all the time. Sorry, but I cannot help him; I cannot bring him happiness. A happy person is never angry. Why, some are even angry at God. What good is that going to do, I ask. Why, if God gets angry he can wipe out an entire village or an entire people like he did in Sodom. That's what I was told when Marianne's father read part of the Bible after dinner one Sunday evening. He was trying to explain to his wife how God works when he's angry. Marianne's mother simply walked away since she didn't want to hear it. She wasn't a Bible reader, she said. So, the husband himself got angry and threw the Bible book at her. It was crazy, I tell you. Anyway, she dodged the book and the book went flying in the living room knocking down the statue of the Virgin Mary. It broke the head and it went rolling on the floor. Marianne went, "Oh no, papa, you beheaded the Blessed Virgin," and she started laughing. Well, that made him even angrier. Anger brings anger; unhappy people cause unhappiness. I bring happiness to those who possess me with feelings that don't hurt anyone. I don't wish to stay with people like Marianne's father. I was glad to move to Maine, I tell you. I wonder if people in Maine ever get angry.

Well, I arrived in Maine on a Monday afternoon on a beautiful September day. The girl who was to have me came up to get me and bring me to her home. I don't know the name of the village or was it a city. I didn't ask. It was a nice home with green shutters and a front door painted yellow. Here we go again, Van Gogh's favorite welcoming color, I said to myself. The girl's name was Gabrielle. People called her Gabbie. She was seventeen years old and loved playing with dolls. She had an entire collection of dolls, large ones, medium sized dolls, small dolls like me and tiny ones that one could put in a teacup. I was so very happy that she loved dolls. That made me feel wanted. I especially liked the doll that was dressed like a dancing queen, all frilly and rich-looking. Why she had a dress made of satin with lace around her sleeves and her neck. She wore some kind of a velvet vest with gold buttons that looked like jewelry to me. She had beautiful blond curly hair with fancy gold-like pins in her hair. Something I always wanted but did not get. I was a poor doll and I did not belong in that kind of society. I really did not care. I wanted to be who I was. Not somebody else. Beautiful clothes and fancy hairdos don't make people and certainly not dolls either. Manufacturers make rich-looking dolls so that they can make huge profits. I'm a cheap doll and that's the way I'll always be. That's just the exterior not the inside where the true essence is. Essence? you may ask. Yes, the essence of being who you truly are. Some people call it soul. Do dolls have that? I don't think so. I don't feel I have one. After all, I'm not human. I was made, not created by a supreme being. That's what I heard someone say one day. It was a man who liked to rant about beings and supreme beings. He called it philosophy. Whatever philosophy is. I remember someone tellling this man that a philosopher was a blind man wearing a blindfold in a dark room telling himself stories about searchers of truth who never found truth but only found tales and stories that people make up when they don't know what to do with themselves. I didn't know what the philosopher was doing in a dark room blindfolded and searcning in the dark for whatever and I never asked why. To me it sounded like an odd story attempting to make fun of philosophers who are looking for truth. What is truth anyways, I wonder. It's the opposite of lies, that's all I know. I am told that many politicians do not know what role truth plays and they fake truth. Yes, they cover up things or rearrange things so that their constituents do not know where matters stand. Either it's the truth or it's untruth. One or the other. It doesn't matter, I'm only a doll. Dolls don't have politicians; they don't need them. We don't play politics and we don't vote. It's better that way. I guess people like politics and they argue about it. All the time. Then there's a winner and a loser, they say. What is that? Winners are not always winning. They lose sometimes. It's all dry and dull to me. I think that philosophers try to explain the workings of the human brain and its product. What product? The product of ideas. Some are great others are simply stupid, I think. Stupid because they don't make sense to other humans and even to dolls like me. I know what stupid is. It's something that goes against reason. Humans are supposed to be reasonable. They're supposed to use their noggin as Garbrielle's father says. By gawd, he's right. Sure, some use it well while others don't know how. If I had a brain I would definitely learn how to use it and not just turn it into a cabbage-like substance. I have nothing against cabbages except I don't like the smell of cooked cabbage. It stinks. So does unused or defamed reason. It stinks to high heaven, I say. Stinks, stinks, stinks. Cabbage reasoning stinks. It ought to be thrown out with the garbage or buried with dead skunks. Everything that stinks should be buried...deep. Maybe lying politicians should be buried too especially when they become crooked, as Gaby's father says. It makes sense, don't you think? I'm just a doll and I can only put my two cents in, as they say. I wonder how much two cents are really worth.

I'm just going off track now. Mmmm, it's nuts. That's it. Let's give it to the squirrels. Haha. Enough of this stupidity, don't you think? I think so.

Let's get back to my story shall we? That's why I'm here with you good people who seek happiness. Well, don't you? I mean doesn't everyone seek happiness one way or another? So, I am what my sticker says, if you possess me I bring happiness. That's some kind of a secret that only I can share with the one who really possesses me. Now, who's going to possess me? I've had several people who somehow possessed me but they did not truly own me as a possession. They only had me for a short time then I was given to someone else. I went from hand to hand, you might say. Well, I'm not done yet. I still have other hands that I need to talk about. It's important if I'm to tell my entire story and how I ended up at the flea market in Paris at the Porte de Clignancourt. Well, here goes.

I am now in another state. It's called Rhode Island. Some people say that it's the smallest state of the entire union. I'll take their word for it. I do not wish to argue with someone who knows more than me. I'm just a doll, after all, a cheap one at that. I wish people would stop calling me that though. I'm really not that cheap. Maybe in price, yes, but not in true worth. Speaking of worth, there is nothing like human worth. I mean the buying and selling of slaves. Last night, our neighbors here, the Waterfords, were talking about the slavery period in the U.S. I did not know there had been one. Interesting. Well, they said that a slave was sold at auction and the proposed buyer always looked at the body parts of the black person, man, woman and even child. They looked at their teeth, their eyes, their hands, their feet and sometimes their XXX, what's in their underwear(I don't have any of that). Terrible thing to do, I say. What does it matter what's inside one's underwear. Humans all have something that's important to each human being, not to everyone who tries to uncover that something. I say that the true worth of any one lays inside the person, not the exterior. A disabled person has it, a blind person has it , a retarded person has it and so on. What am I worth? Truly? I'm worth so many centimes but my true worth is my sticker. What I bring to the one who possesses me. That's what the sticker says. I just wish I can bring a lot of happiness to that one. It's going to happen but when and to whom, I don't know. It's a mystery just like happiness is.

Rhode Island is a place where people love dolls, I found out. From my own observations, I mean. I don't know if it's true but so far I think it is so because so many people seem to love me and I feel wanted. That's the true test of the pudding, as they say. I think that's what people say. People come out with all kinds of things, all kinds of sayings. It makes me blink my eyes. I can, you know, just like I can move my arms and my legs. Not my feet. That's alright. I was created, no, I was made that way. Some dolls even have an opening in their mouths for someone to put the tip of a suce/nipple in it and simulate the drinking of milk or formula. Isn't that keen? I don't have that. I tell you, I'm the simplest and least endowed of all dolls. I don't want to be bottle-fed. I don't need it. What I need is to be wanted. To be wanted means to be loved. That's the most important part of my existence. I just loved Marianne. She used to tell me over and over again."Ma poupée, ma petite charmante de poupée, je t'aime tu sais"/My doll, my charming little doll I love you, you know. That really sent me reeling off to another planet. It's true, you know, the gift of expressed love can send one to outer space, into the stars where starlight turns you to golden syrup on a hot pancake that your mother hands over to you in the morning. Oh, I wish I could taste and eat such a breakfast. Yes, Marianne was a favorite of mine.She knew how to express her true love, as true as the heart can be. I'm sorry if I sound romantic and so easily dramatic about it but that's me, Founie, the simplest of dolls. I'm not a simpleton for sure, but I am a very simple doll who expresses truth and honest feelings the best I can by making little girls and people too feel my honest presence oftentimes without words, just warm cozy feelings that come out in the form of a smile, the wink of an eye or simply by the touch of the little finger. You see, little fingers were made for this, touch the heart without touching the bones or the flesh of a human being. Sounds crazy, doesn't it? Well, it's not. Little fingers are created to touch each other and touch the bright spots of the heart. Anyone's heart, girls, boys, women's even grown men. Grown men's hearts are usually the hardest to touch since they're made of tough and sinewy fibers that makes them not too sensitive to anything. Not all men, but so many men. I don't know why. Now you're going to say that science does not prove that. I agree but it doesn't disprove the fact that men are not as sensitive and soft in feelings. Is it because men don't have the softness of little girls, I really mean the softness of being. The softness of knowing how to treat others even cats, dogs, and dolls. However, there are some little girls who grow up to be tough and heart-hardened. So many of them want so much to be at the same level as men. they want to have the same privileges and the same excuses to be as violent as men. Does violence make anyone genuine or really real? But how does one show softness? By touching delicately and with true honesty and deep sensitivity one's deep feelings, when they are above board. Am I being too delicately sensitive or crazily romantic about feelings? Well, I might be but that's my doll's way of expressing what I feel and what I sense is happening in the human world of inter-connecting or dissolving into robots or mechanical creations. Yes, people do create/make robots and sometimes people turn into robots so mechanical have they become. I mean they are without human ways of expressing themselves. I suppose one would have to define the term human. I'll let people do that. They know better than me. I'm a doll.

The family I lived with in Providence, Rhode Island had the name of Riomaldi. They were of Italian heritage and customs. A real loving and a touchy-touchy family, I may add. I liked that. There were seven family members. The mother was the core or heart while the father was the bread-winner and solid member on which all the members relied. He was their rock, their strong support. Of course, not all of them liked his temper and his violent outbursts, but he always returned to his much softer side. Then he was much much more understanding as a father, as a husband and even as an uncle and a friend. His name was Umberto. The wife's name, Isofina. The little girl to whom I was confided, her name was Constanza Maria Isabella Riomaldi. Why so many names, I asked myself Some families, I may even add, so many ethnic groups, prefer a lot of names given to someone since it represents an attachment to roots. Roots are important, explained to me Umberto, for without roots a tree dies. So does a family, he said. I didn't have roots but I did have a sticker. That was enough for me.

I just loved the family's way of doing things like when they had meals together. There was talking, sharing the recent news, giving compliments and, of course, food. All was done with courtesy and love. I could see it and taste it. It was great. I enjoyed it. Each one had the delight of being who he or she was. Individuality, I called it. No one would have dared to erase it by stomping on it or defacing it with ugly words. I found it marvelous. Even the cat, Thumbelina, was included in their everyday get-together over food. Oh, the food! It looked scrumptious. There was all kinds of pasta, sauces, cheeses, breads and, of course, wines. It was a smack-your-lips event each time. I could see it. Constanza very often took me in her hands and put me in the large pocket of her apron. Her mother made her wear an apron all the time."To keep good and nice clothes clean," she said. Constanza was a nice girl, an obedient child and she loved her mother very much. Her mother used to tell her, "Make sure you take that doll out of your pocket before I put your apron in the wash because the poor doll will go bonanza in the water and soap. You certainly don't want that." One time Constanza did forget me in her apron pocket(I don't know why she kept me there, really) and her mother fortunately retrieved me and gave me back to the girl with black curly hair. Yes, she had very pretty hair, a very lovely face and hands that were white as marble. She kept them that way. Constanza was a sight to see when she was all dolled up(that's what people say when a girl is presentable). However, she was a little too proud of herself and showed signs of being haughty and overbearing. She would keep after her father to get his attention until he told her to stop it. He had had enough of her and her girly intensions. I don't know why she acted that way. Her mother never minded Constanza's flattery and childish behavior. She was a child after all, she said.

Sometimes, I asked myself if Constanza truly wanted me or not. She certainly did not pay too much attention to me, her borrowed doll. Always in her apron pocket. I was glad when she stepped out with her parents, then I would be on her night table next to a pretty lamp that shed a pinkish light. I missed having someone around me listening to their babbling and shuffling around. It was so stimulating for me. I loved people, people who are entertaining and joyful. Most of the time they were if Constanza allowed me to be there. After all, they were Italians, people of great and lively personalities. Just like the French. Oh, how I loved Marianne's people, especially Marianne herself, such a lively and warm person, she was, and very careful to include me everywhere she went. Never in a pocket also. Constanza could have learned a lot from Marianne. I miss her beaucoup.

I didn't stay too long at the Riomaldis, although I liked Rhode Island and its nice people in general. I loved the flowers there. They were colorful and sweet to the eyes, mine when I opened them. Then I was sent to a little girl named Évangéline in Nova Scotia. I was told that the area where I was staying had a large population of Acadians. Acadians are French-speaking whose ancestors were the first ones to come to the soil of la Nouvelle-France. Many of them have their own way of speaking called the chiac. I couldn't get used to it but I realized I wasn't one of theirs. Of course, Évangéline was. What a nice and pleasant girl she was. I could tell she really wanted me. Moi, a doll. She wanted to adopt me she told her mother, but the mother told her she couldn't since she was only borrowed. Borrowing means returning, said the mother. "But I want her," said the little girl. That warmed my heart I could have cried. Being wanted is so great a feeling when one feels lonely and far away from home wherever home is.

Évangéline shared a lot with me. People thought she talked to a dumb doll but I did listen and understood her when she talked to me alone in her bedroom sitting on a padded stool next to a window with lace curtains. The sun just shined through them and made lace-like patterns on the floor. I loved it. The little girl told me that her name Évangéline came from a very old story about the Acadians and a girl with that name. That she and her lover, Gabriel, had a very difficult time to stay together because the British were after the Acadians and their land. Since the Acadians refused to do what the British wanted them to do, sign a paper that would indicate they were going to be loyal to the crown, they were deported to strange lands and many were separated from their own. I believe it was called the Grand Dérangement. Awful, awful thing to happen to people. Why were they taken away from their peaceful and tranquil land, the little girl could not tell. All she knew was that it happened. Well, poor Évangéline of the story ended up in Louisiana and hunted for her lover Gabriel, only to find him sick and dying. Poor things, such a sad story. How cruel can people be, I thought. Some Acadians returned to their native soil and some of them even came to northern Maine.

YOUNIE, THE FLEA MARKET DOLL

I was in Nova Scotia in a town called Paquetteville. People were very lively in Paquetteville. They knew how to have fun. I was brought to many parties and dances there. Not in a pocket but up front in little Évangéline's hands. People she met usually asked her what was the doll's name and she would reply that I did not have one but that she would give me one when she could. In the meantime, I was the doll with no name. A "younie" some said and the name stuck to me. What in the world does "younie" mean, I said to myself. I found out that it came from a little boy who once said younie when he was trying to connect you and me and babbled "younie". That word stuck as people laughed and used it to mean someone closely connected to someone else or something else. I take it to mean wanting and being wanted. You know, closeness and being loved. You and me, "younie." I grew to love that name. That's the one that stuck to me like my sticker. "Younie" brings happiness; closeness brings happiness is what I think. But I'm just a doll. Que voulez-vous? as they say in France. What do you want?

I stayed with Évangéline six months, longer if I had my wish granted. However, I truly and sincerely loved my stay in the land of Évangéline. There's even a song about her. I would sing it to you but I don't have a voice. You can hear it almost anywhere where good Acadian music is sung especially at parties. As I said, Acadians have lots of parties. They're party-loving people.

In the meantime, I met a cute little boy by the name of Robbie. His full name was Robert Ernest Lapierre jr. They all called him Robbie and they all loved him as far as I could tell. However, Évangéline whispered to me that the poor little Robbie was very sick. He had cancer. He was going to die. His parents did everything they could but everything failed. Everything they could afford since they were poor. People had a fundraiser for the family but that wasn't enough. The parish church had a bean supper and gave all the proceeds to the Lapierre family and that was not enough, enough to pay for expensive treatments. So, they did their best to keep Robbie comfortable and in the least pain. The poor boy never complained. He never cried. He never ever said that he wanted to die. Rather, he wanted to live. I could tell. His mother took very very good care of him. bathing him, rocking him in the old family rocking chair, and telling him stories about animals and other children that had recovered from illnesses and deadly diseases. He only once asked his mother if he was going to recover from his maladie and his mother told him she did not really know but that everyone was praying for him to recover. I did the best I knew how to pray. I had never learned.

Robbie taught me how to pray. How does one teach a doll how to pray, you might ask. Well, it begins with a communication through heart-wishing. Heart-wishing? Yes, heart-wishing by making sure your heart feelings are in line with someone else's heart. It's done by wishing and wishing and wishing until you can feel it. Feel what, you might say. Feel that you are connected. Hearts can be connected. Really? Yes, connected by feelings and the willingness to be connected. It's like magic. No one can truly explain it. It happens. Anyways, I made it happen when I knew that Robbie wanted me and wanted my feelings to be connected to his. There was some kind of a spark then. I knew it, Robbie knew it. When a spark like that happens then you can see a shooting star happening in the night sky. Robbie saw it and shouted to his mother that he had seen a shooting star. He was waiting for Évangéline to bring me to him since he wanted me and I wanted him. Évangéline used to bring me to his house every day just to console him and make him feel better. That day once we had connected together, we began to talk to one another. I don't mean to talk like humans ordinarily do but doll talk. You know silent but feeling talk.

Robbie told me that he knew he was going to die and that people's prayers were being answered because he was not sad neither lonely nor terrified. Love and wanting love and kindness was what took care of him and his maladie. I told him what makes people sick was a lack of understanding and a lack of being wanted. Human beings react to that and their body react in turn. In some cases it's worse, like having cancer. He told me he understood but he was worried about his parents who suffered terrible fright and awful worries about him. "Please tell them not to worry so much. Tell them I'll be fine once I get to a place beyond the stars where there is ever and ever quiet peace and no more suffering. My heart is going to melt into the heart of Jesus. His mother will see to it," he told me. But how will I get to communicate to your parents? I asked him. "You'll know how," he said, and he fell asleep.

The only way I could communicate with Robbie's parents was through Évangéline. I told her what I wanted them to hear and she communicated it to them. At first, they did not know how to respond to it but Évangéline told them that it was doll's talk, and they believed her. Anyways, they seemed to be consoled. Except, one night, Robbie's mother heard a loud shriek from little Robbie's room. She rushed to his bedside and saw that the poor child was in tears. He seemed frightened. His eyes were wide and filled with that terrible fright that unknown sources bring to humans, especially at night. She sat on the bed and tried very hard to cast off the fright but poor Robbie was so frightened that he uttered he did not want to go to sleep anymore. He was afraid of sleep and the dark. The evil forces were out to get him."What evil forces", asked the mother. "You know the ones that the doll brought to me here." Then he suddenly fell back to sleep.

"What evil forces did I bring to him?" I asked Évangéline. "What could possibly make him say that? I never in my existence as a poor doll would have ever frightened poor little boy Robbie. Never, never, never." I just could not understand what was happening. I did not know or played with forces of evil. I knew they existed but I did not even know what they were. I was as innocent as little Robbie was. I guess that forces of evil go after the innocent ones. They want to crush their willingness to thrive in the wanting of one another's love and sharing of it. Innocence to me is the lack of bad or terrifying feelings that come to harm the heart and render it incapable to trust in themselves and in others. I'm a doll, I do not know everything.

What was worse, was the fact that Robbie's mother had heard directly from her son that I was the evil bringer. I was the bad one who curses little children with my presence and my talk whatever that was. So, I was told to leave by Évangéline since she had no other choices but to ban me forever from the Acadian soil and its people, the good and party-going people. The people I got to love. The people that gave me the name, "Younie." The sad thing was that I was not the one who was responsible in frightening little Robbie. Outside forces did that. Probably his cancer. Who knows? Crazy things happen to people. Crazy things happen to dolls too. So, I left early in the morning even before the sunrise so that people could not see my leaving and shout, "Burn that damn thing. It's probably a voodoo doll, a curse on us Acadians. We had enough of it. Enough of one big dérangement. Out with the evil one.

Out. Out. nevermore." So, I felt I had my own grand dérangement since I was shoved away, unwanted and undesired. That's an awful feeling inflicted on someone even though I was only a simple doll. .

I was transported outside of town to the train station where someone I did not know boarded with me and off we went to some place I did not want to go. Why? Because I knew deep inside my reputation was being marred by lies and that whoever would get me would definitely not want me. Not at all. Here I lay in someone's bag practically choking next to a banana and a ripe pear that I could not and did not want to eat. It was a very lonely trip back to Maine. Yes, that's where they took me whoever they were. Once in Maine they told someone in charge that I would be going to Mexico. Far, far away. Mexico? I said to myself. Why I don't even speak Spanish.

If anyone wanted to get rid of me, that was the place, I guess. Far far away. Far from France, far from Canada and far from New England where I had met some nice people and who most of them wanted me. Anyway, I had to get used to it. I was a doll and I was in the custody of humans. Dolls cannot manage their own affairs certainly not even their existence. I was at the mercy of fate and circumstances. Do you know what fate is? I do. It's a thing or circumstance that rules your existence and your future. It's what is going to happen to you and you do not know about it. It happens, that's all. People have fate to rule over them and determine what's going to happen to them and so do dolls. You did not know that did you? Writers write about the tragedy of fate and its consequences. They sometimes call it fatality or destiny. Look for it. Read some books and try to find it. It's there. I know. I don't read but I learn through human and doll sharing. Dolls are not stupid, I'll have you know.

Now, let me see where I'm at in my story. Oh yes, Mexico. Why was I sent there and by whom? Well, the reason I was sent there is because little Robbie's mother wanted me out of there, out of her sight and out of her son's presence completely. She was afraid of me and my presence since she believed I was an evil presence in Robbie's life. Robbie through his nightmare had told her so and she believed him. After all, he was her son. Why would she not believe him? Even though she did not bother to investigate the whole thing. She had seen how frightened her son was. She herself became frightened, so much so that her life seemed utterly filled with fear from that moment on.She absolutely did not WANT me there. A doll, think of it. To her I had turned out to be a voodoo doll of some kind. Dangerous and scary. I didn't blame her but I could not remain there either. I cannot stay with someone who does not want me. I made that clear before and I will persist in my belief and my feeling of wanted to belong and be wanted.

So, they called Rose-Hélène in Canada and she contacted Marianne in France who made the connection in Mexico. Marianne had a few well-known connections there especially in Oaxaca. So it was arranged that a good friend she knew in Maine was contacted directly and he agreed to pick me up and fly me to Mexico with all expenses paid. He would be my chaperone. That's one way of putting things. Me a doll with a chaperone, my gawd!

I did not know where exactly I was going, at first, and I did not know the man who came to get me, but I had no choice in the matter. It was as though I was being kidnapped. That's the way I felt. I wanted to say goodbye to little Robbie but the mother refused adamantly. No! No! No! She kept repeating. I bet you that he cried when he heard I was not going to return to see him. Never. I wanted to cry myself. I could not. I was a doll. There are many things a doll cannot do but wish they had the power to do it. That's the life of a doll, I tell you. It's sometimes frustrating, I'll have you know. Well, I'm a doll and I will remain a doll, that I know. At times I want to celebrate my life as a doll and shout with joy that I am a human-made creation, not created but made by human hands. You know what I mean. I don't have to explain it to you again. You're bright enough to get it, don't you?

The stranger's name was Albert and he was an older guy with a mustache. He had a very strong French accent and he sang happy songs in French while we traveled. Unfortunately, the stewardess did not allow him to sing out loud. It would disturb the other passengers, she told him. "Oui, Mademoiselle, he told her. He then fell asleep in his seat while I was stuck in his carry-on bag in the upper loft. It felt somewhat uncomfortable but I got used to it. After all, I'm a doll and dolls have to get used to a lot of things like being shoved around and sent somewhere without consent or knowledge. I'm not dumb. I know when I'm being shipped off somewhere where unwanted guests are taken in without being at all wanted or called for. Certainly not desired. I know. I know all too well. I could tell you that it hurts, but I cannot communicate directly with you. I'd have to do it some other way like that mysterious communication line that I told you about. Anyways, I had to accept and respect the hand that was offered to me. That was Albert's hand of mercy, I call it. Lordy lord, he was a patient and merciful man that one. He took care that I wasn't abused or stolen. People saw that he put a doll in his travel bag when they were checking his luggage and passport. I did not carry any of that. I was but a doll. Some people could have swiped me away when he wasn't looking, you know. But he was vigilant and I say merciful. I survived the plane ride. Before we deplaned, as they say in the plane business, he checked inside his bag to see that I was still there. With my moveable eyes I winked at him but he did not notice it. I meant, I'm O.K. Founie says I'm O.K.

We landed in Mexico City and WOW, there was a lot of of people at that airport. Lots and lots of travelers. Where did they all come from, I asked myself. Well, it's a big world and there are so many people coming and going. No one can keep track of them. Once we got to customs we were faced with an officer who asked Albert if he was traveling with anyone or with anything dangerous like harmful drugs. "Non, Monsieur, rien de dangereux, seulement la poupée de bonheur"./only the happiness doll, and he smiled. That made the officer smile too. The officer then said, " Si, senor" and waved us bye. Albert had taken me out of his bag and was carrying me in his right hand. Some kids saw what he had in his hand and smiled while others stopped to take a look at me. Some parents prevented their children from doing that. Well, they just turned around and kept looking at Albert and me. I guess that they had never seen a happiness doll before. I don't know. I could sense that the children wanted me or desired to come closer to me but they could not. However, that made me feel good. It's so good to feel wanted. I know, I know I shouldn't keep saying that but I can't stop myself. To want and to feel wanted, that is the big question to me. It will never leave me and I will never quite leave it. It's very important and I take seriously important things and specially questions. Don't you do the same? If you don't, then there's something wrong with you. That, coming from a doll that's not stupid. Period.

Albert and I left the airport and did not go directly to Oaxaca. He wanted to visit Mexico City and especially the basilica of Our Lay of Guadalupe and see the tilma with the imprint of Our Lady of Guadalupe that Juan Diego had presented to the bishop as proof of Our Lady appearing to him up on the hill. Albert explained all of the matter of Guadalupe to an American stranger who was asking people about it but could not find anyone to do so in English. That's when I found out about this Guadalupe matter. That's what I called it. Well, it goes like this.

It was a miraculous apparition to a peasant named Juan Diego. He was a poor man living with his uncle up in the hillside area. He wore simple clothes with a tilma around his shoulders to protect him from cold weather. It was his mantle made out of vegetable fibers. There were more than one apparition. Our Lady asked him to tell the bishop that a shrine be made right there on the hillside in her honor. In return, the bishop asked for proof of this and Juan Diego later returned carrying in his mantle Castillian roses not native to Mexican soil. When he opened his mantle, roses fell out of it and the image of Our Lady of Guadalupe appeared. That image is still fresh and is enshrined in the basilica. Millions of people from all over the world have come to the basilica to see the miraculous image. It is venerated by all Mexican believers as well as those of Spanish origins in several countries. It's a very important venerated shrine and people flock to it all the time. Our Lady of Guadalupe has become the patroness of these people and, of course, of Mexico itself. Why they have pictures of the image in houses, hotels, in churches and even in bars. "Can you believe this?" asked Albert to the American stranger. A doll like me is not a believer in miracles but I, Younie, do believe what Albert told the stranger. I believe it's absolutely incredibly true. I feel it in my body and in my feelings as a doll. What can I tell you?

We left Mexico City and headed for Oaxaca where Albert was supposed to bring me to someone who had four children, one of which was a young girl named Maria Gonsalva. I told myself, here we go again. We're going to meet yet another young girl and she may or may not be a wanting person. You know what I mean don't you? Well, let me continue my story.

Albert and I took a bus to go to Oaxaca. It was full. There were two boys sitting right in front of us and they were very boistrous, as they say. They jumped, they talked out loud and even shouted things I would not repeat. They were absolutely hateful. The parents did not seem to care. They let them fool around like that. That's what Albert told the mother of the little girl that was getting me. It was indeed a long ride and I knew that Albert would be tired. So when we got to Oaxaca, the first thing Albert did was to get a room at a small hotel and take a nap before going to see the family of the little girl. I just lay there in his bag waiting to be taken out. Finally, Albert woke up, went to the bathroom, combed his hair and washed his face, and off we went to the address given him. It was a small street on the west side of the city. There were small children playing in the street. Two boys kept yelling something in Spanish. I did not know what they were shouting but I did feel it wasn't good. It sounded bad and nasty to me. Albert just smiled and asked one of the children where number twelve was, numero doce. They all pointed to a house across the street that seemed somewhat delapidated. The people living there had to be poor. I could feel it. I was shaken and thought that I would not be well received. Not that I did not like poor people but sometimes they can be the unwanting kind. I was wrong.

    The family was ever so kind to me, both parents, Estivo and Amelia, and the four children were of the wanting kind, I could tell. Maria Gonsalva was cute as a button with shiny black hair, deep dark eyes with long eyelashes that made her look like a movie star, and she had the warmest smile I've ever seen on a child's face. I was bursting with satisfaction. Dolls do sometimes, you know.

    It wasn't easy for me to really get to know the little girl to whom I was confided since she was shy and spoke only Spanish, But we got along with my learning some Spanish words such as hola, adios, gracias, amor, and si for yes. Oh, I was forgetting, doll in Spanish is muneca with a tilde on the "n". You know, a little wavy accent mark. There I taught you something. Each day I learned something. I learned that Mexican food can be much appreciated when one is hungry whether one likes it or not. But of course everyone in Mexico likes Mexican food. As a doll, I do not eat anything, so food means nothing to me, only to humans who love to eat. Little Maria Gonsalva relished her food. I could see it and feel it. I must tell you that it did not take too long for the two of us to communicate. She was all wired up for it. I mean she was naturally open to doll talk, if you know what I mean. Feeling talk. For some humans it takes time while others like Maria in no time she knew how and what to communicate with me, Younie, the flea market doll. I am a strange creature to many. I should not say creature since I was not created. I was made, fabricated, you know homo faber, as I explained before. Let's forget that part. It's not too interesting anyways.

I could tell you all the things Maria and I did and all the feelings we shared together but that would take up a lot of your time and mine too. Let's just say that I enjoyed being with Maria Gonsalva. My journey with people was my first one and I was made to feel happy since I was bringing happiness to the one who would possess me. That I knew. My sticker said so. Marianne had told me so by repeating that I was une porteuse de bonheur, a carrier of happiness. I brought or I was bringing happiness and that was quite the job I had. Not every doll has a task like mine. They don't all have stickers except the sticker price. I didn't have one. At least, I don't remember. By the way happiness in Spanish is felicidad. Felicidad, felicidad everybody! Soy la portadora de la felicidad. I am the bearer of happiness, I'll have you know. That's what I'll tell everybody who understands me.

Not the bearer of good news, la portadora de buenas noticias, but of happiness, la FELICIDAD! wow! Put that in your pipe and smoke it, as my old uncle Ned used to say. Uncle Ned was and still is my imaginary relative. Sometimes I have to make some up since I don't know of anybody else. That's what dolls do. Make up things and people. It's fun. Try it sometimes.

Well, here are some of the more interesting things that Maria and I enjoyed doing. I know that I have to give some kind of account of my doings if I'm going to tell my story. So here goes. Maria had many aunts and uncles and she saw or visited them quite often. All of them lived not too far. Maria's father had an old car that he used for his errands . He did most of the repair work on it when it needed it. He was a good mechanic and that's how he earned money by doing small jobs for neighbors on their cars. He did not earn much money, but he earned enough to survive. His wife used to tell him that they needed more pesos now and then when she ran out of her own money. She did the laundry for others. Estivo, the husband, Maria's father, went around the neighborhood and asked people for jobs. He had a hard time finding work, but occasionally he did get one that paid him well enough to replenish his wife's coffers. She was happy then. The children would go begging for coins around town but their father used to tell them to stop it for they were not poor beggars. They did not beg for coins nor for food. They earned it, he said. He was a very proud man as far as I could see. Maria used to tell me that. Her father was a proud hombre.

Estivo knew this man who dealt with some kind of drug and made money selling it. His wife used to warn Estivo about getting involved with Tomas, the drug dealer, she called him. Although a very honest man, Estivo sometimes looked the other way and went to visit Tomas when he thouhgt his friend had an adventurous opportunity ahead of him. Estivo loved adventures. He did not care about drugs; he simply loved adventures and the fun they brought.

One day Tomas told Estivo about an adventure that was coming up and wanted to know if Estivo wanted to join him. Estivo did not hesitate in saying si, that's yes in Spanish. The yes meant that the two compadres would be going up to the mountains of Oaxaca at a place called Huautla where there was an old woman called Maria Sabrina who dealt with mushrooms that were known as the sacred mushrooms by many. These mushrooms brought special visions that aroused the soul, Maria Sabrina told people who wanted to find out more about her healing. You see she was a curandera, a healer. Over the years she had learned much about her roots that were part of her being Mazatec. People said that her healing skills were mystical and that famous people from everywhere came to see her and participate in her healing ceremonies that she called veladas/vigils. They were always done at night under the stars. It was said that the hippies found out about her and her mysterious mushrooms that had special mind-blowing powers and started coming to her place in the Sierra mountains. It was said that Bob Dylan as well as John Lennon had gotten involved with this so-called sacred ritual. Her neighbors did not like it since they considered it an invasion of privacy. All those strangers putting their noses into their village and their business. They warned Maria Sabrina not to let strangers come into Huautla. However, people continued coming to see her just to get some of her "medicine" or mushrooms. She had become famous, people said.

Well, that's the woman that Tomas was going to pay a visit with Estivo. He wanted some of those mushrooms. He did not want to participate in a vigil of healing, he told his friend. He only wanted to get some sacred mushrooms and sell them for profit. And he told Estivo that he would share his profit with him. Well, that made Estivo happy. Yes, an adventure in the mountains and some money. How could he refuse. All he had to do was drive up there and go to Huautla where Maria Sabrina lived. Unfortunately the car broke down in the middle of the trip and Estivo could not get it working. He tried and tried but the car would not start. Tomas got angry at him and shouted that Estivo was no good with cars and that he was bad luck to him. Estivo, usually a kind and peace-loving man got angry too and the two friends started throwing punches at one another. Estivo hit Tomas with a wrench and he fell to the ground unconscious. He could not revive him. He was dead. Flat dead on the road.

Finally, Estivo ran to the nearest village and got help. There was no hospital and although they tried to help Tomas, it was impossible to bring him back to life and the local village officer blamed Estivo for Tomas's death. He called it murder.

Estivo was terribly shaken by what was happening. He was being accused of a crime he had not committed. He could not defend himself. He did not know how. He was put in jail. He would have to go to trial for his crime. Sure, he had hit Tomas with a wrench but it was not a crime, he told the police. The worst part was that they found a bag of drugs hidden in the back seat of the car and told Estivo that he was part of a drug related offense besides the murder. That really racked Estivo's brain and he began raving and shouting terrible things until they branded him a vicious insane offender of the law.

Well, the wife, Amelia, was located and she was brought to the village where her husband was. She found that her husband had gone mad, crazy over all the insults, the blame and offenses thrown at him. There was nothing she could do about it. Estivo was carted away to an insane asylum never to be seen again. Amelia went back home took her three children and me to her godparents house and lived there working very hard at odd jobs to help support the people she loved and cared for. For you see godparents are responsible for their godchildren in Mexico and that is why Amelia went to live with them. They were two elderly, kind, loving persons. I found them "wanting" if you know what I mean. They wanted Amelia and her children. They even wanted me, a poor doll in a strange country. That's the story Maria told me and all the details she got to know. Maria and I communicated well together. I thought she was a very nice girl and a loving and giving girl. I was so sad about the father. The mother too. Sad to have bad luck like that. Too bad that Estivo liked adventures as he did because that was a very sad and terrible adventure he had on the way to the mountains with his friend Tomas, the shady friend I would call him. Shady because I thought he was not a very nice amigo to begin with. I guess you could call this part of my story the bad luck episode.

I left Maria Gonsalva and Mexico when the mother received a telegram telling her that I was going to be picked up by another friend of Marianne. Her name was Annabelle LeMaire. She lived in Belgium. You see I travelled all over the place wherever Marianne sent me. I took her word for it and never questioned her decisions. She knew what she was doing and I trusted her. I was only a doll after all. A simple flea market doll with a sticker. I thought my sticker would fall off after so many moves and travels, but no it was still there. It's still on now. Dieu merci, as the French say. French is always with me and I get better at it every day it seems. Anyhow, I was going to yet another country that spoke French, la Belgique.

Belgium is further up from France and it is a very nice country I heard say. The city where I went to was called Mons and it was next to the town of Binche where the festival of Gilles took place every year right before Ash Wednesday. Annabelle told me all about it. She truly loved this festival as many other people loved it, she said. Annabelle was a lovely young lady with beautiful brown eyes and a very nice complexion. She had lovely hands white as snow. I felt comfortable in them. I noticed that she took very good care of her fingernails. You see even if I am a doll, I notice things. Annabelle was

YOUNIE, THE FLEA MARKET DOLL

around fifteen years old and she attracted young men who loved her charm and beauty, but she would have none of them. You see, she was not quite ready for un ami de coeur/ a friend of the heart, she confided to me. Yes, I had a very nice communication line with her. She was indeed of the wanting kind if you know what I mean. She loved nice clothes and genuine leather shoes. Her father called her une demoiselle de haute couture/a high fashion young lady. She smiled and blushed a bit when her father told her that. I could tell that the father loved his daughter. The father's name was Gilles Arthur. Annabelle's mother died when she was but seven years old. Her grandmother, Aurore, brought her up with the father's demand that his mother take over the task of bringing up his child. Annabelle loved her grandmother, Aurore. She spoiled her rotten but Aurore explained that was because children without mothers deserve extra care and love. I then realized that the grandmother was really a wanting kind. I love them these wanting kinds. I'm just a doll but I just love being wanted, as you already know.

It was around the time of year when Lent was fast approaching and as Annabelle told her grandmother it would be time for the Gilles Festival. What was that, I asked Annabelle. Well, she started explaining to me what it was all about when her grandmother interrupted her and asked her to please go upstairs to her room and finish her home assignments. You see, Annabelle was still in school and teachers assigned homework. It was the usual thing. Teachers care about students learning and so they give them home assigments to bolster their academic pursuits. It's simply a reasonable thing to do if one is interested in a student's progress. I learned that a long time ago. You see, I spent a lot of time with students who were my so-called owners, short spell owners of course.

Coming back to the festival, here is what Annabelle told me. She was all excited about it because she just loved the festival of clowns, as she called them. The Gilles Festival features men dressed up in bright costumes and wear wax masks with goggle-type glasses with eyes and a long curling mustache. They have a large red dot on their chins. On their chests there is a large sleigh-ride type bell. There are many of these men who get dressed up for this festival, Annabelle said. They simply love to have fun in the streets. They sing songs, they shout and have fun with the population who is awaiting the forty-day season of Lent when fun is lowered to a degree of sacrifices and penance. That's what Annabelle told me. I knew what Lent was and I knew about Mardi Gras in New Orleans but I did not know about the Gilles Festival in Belgium. Furthermore, I was told that in colonial Quebec, people would go outside and from door to door banging on pots and pans and make loud noises as a prelude to the coming of Lent. Of course, people would give the so-called celebrants food and drink. You cannot have a celebration without that. Everyone knows that.

Another folklore happening in Belgium is the feast of Saint Nicholas. In the States they call him Santa Claus. Well, in Belgium, children take out their shoes and place them near the hearth and put in them either water ot wine for Saint Nicholas who brings them presents. Oh yes, they also leave a carrot for Saint Nicholas' donkey or horse whichever he comes with. I love their customs and I'm hoping to see more of them.

Annabelle had a distant cousin by the name of Eddy Merckx. He was the most celebrated cyclist in the country, she told me. He had won five Tour de France. She was very proud of him as were most people in Belgium. I did not get to meet him but I heard a lot about him. I only wish I could pedal a bike. I'd run in a race too, a doll race. I can't even move my feet. I'm that kind of a doll, you know.

There are other famous people in Belgium such as Jacques Brel. He's dead now; he died young. His famous and popular song was "Ne me quitte pas." I don't know if you remember that. It's a sad song about someone leaving someone who begs that someone not to leave him or her, I supppose. So many singers sang that song like Barbra Streisand. Annabelle told me that her father used to play that song on his CD player. "I suppose", she said, "it it was about my mother leaving him in death. My father grieved my mother for a very long time. He never remarried."

Also, there is the famous Belgian detective, Hercule Poirot created for the mystery novels that Agatha Christie wrote. He became quite famous as an astute detective. She created him that way. Annabelle did not care too much about Agatha Christie's detective stories. She much preferred romances, she told me. She especially liked the medieval romances with knights and ladies in waiting such as Lancelot and Queen Guenevere. She loved the Romeo and Juliette romance. Why? Because they were young people in love, she said. "They were not allowed to get together since the two families fought them and their wanting to be in each other's arms. See, another story about wanting. Wanting is so very important. I keep telling you that. Believe me when I say that wanting is the first step of love and loving. You can't love someone who does not want you. You can be infatuated with someone but it does not mean love, genuine love. It means infatuation, fat love, I call it. Not real love at all.

You might want me to talk about Belgian cuisine, don't you? Well, there are some dishes that are worth talking about. There's, of course, French fries, waffles, and not to forget chocolate. Belgian chocolate is famous all over the world like Lady Godiva and Heuhaus chocolates. I'm so sorry that I cannot even taste it. They tell me that it's the best."Le meilleur chocolat du monde!" Oh, my gawd! I feel deprived. However, I can live without chocolate. Do I have a life? What kind of life? A life of wanting to be wanted, that's my life and of course apporter le bonheur à qui me possède/ bring happiness to whoever possesses me. It's not only my goal but my life as a doll. Who would have thought that a doll would and could bring happiness. Well, someone did since I'm wearing a sticker about happiness. That sticker is my soul, my reason for living if I live, not as a human being but as a doll. I suppose dolls have lives in a certain way. Living is exisiting and I certainly exist.

I suppose my story in Belgium is but a kind of documentary but it tells you about things you might not have known. Right? I see it as being woven in my story. Stories without some cultural features are somewhat dull and without some aspects of what is considered genuine human values, I suppose. I like to think of it in that sense. I may be wrong but I don't think so. What would human lives be without cultural values, I wonder. But, I'm just a doll, remember?

I left Mons when Annabelle's grandmother passed away. She was eighty-eight years old. She had a good life and a generous one at that. She truly was a wanting spirit and it showed. I grieved with Annabelle and her father. Grieving is a call from the heart, a call of remembering the good and bad times shared by people who are close to one another. The pangs are deep and at times merciless, but they're feelings of love, deep and heartfelt love of the wanting kind. You know what I mean, don't you?

Aurore was buried next to her husband who was a chocolatier of first class, Annabelle told me. He once made a special batch of heart-shaped chocolates for his wife and he gave it to her on their anniversary. She ate one and put the rest away. She never touched the rest of them until she felt that death was fast approaching and she told her son and granddaughter they were going to celebrate. "Celebrate what" asked Annabellle. "Well I feel it's time for me to depart from you and this earth of ours and I want to celebrate my going home to Edmond(that was her husband's name). I want to celebrate, that's all. I want us to celebrate my homegoing where chocolate abounds and the taste is so good. The chocolate of heaven, my dears." So the three of them had a piece of heart-shaped chocolate. It tasted absolutely good, rich, smooth and heart -felt," Annabelle told me afterwards. The rest was put away by the father who was another wanting person, All he ever wanted was to be close to his family especially his dear sweet mother and to his daughter, Annabelle. Closeness is a good part of the wanting feature. I believe I have already told you that. If not, well here it is for you to digest. You have a stomach, well, digest in goodness and delight.

My next locale was to be Haiti. Why Haiti? you might ask. Well I'm going to tell you all about it right now. Suffice it to say that I obey all commands made by Marianne like it or not. What is there not to like if you trust someone and desire to please that someone you want to keep loving and respecting her wishes? Tell me. I know what you are going to say. Well, before you tell me something, I'm going to continue my story, my flea market doll story. It's my reason for being, my journey and discovery of the human wanting. Do you get it?

Haiti is way down in the Caribbean islands. It was a long trip for me and my companion, Antoine Desautels. Antoine came from a small town in the province of Quebec. He was a close friend of Marianne. They had attended a couple of conferences together when Marianne was studying the creole language and literature. I'll talk to you about that later.

YOUNIE, THE FLEA MARKET DOLL

We arrived in Port-au-Prince late on a Monday afternoon. It was hot and humid. I could see that poor Antoine was sweating and found the weather artocious. He wasn't used to this kind of humidity. "Il fait trop chaud et humide, je ne suis pas habitué à cela"/ It's too hot and humid and I'm not used to it, he said to the customs officer who greeted us. The officer simply smiled. I was laying down in Antoine's carry-on bag that happened to be opened and I could see the customs officer since my eyes were opened. I was fine because I did not feel the heat nor the humidity. I'm a doll.

Antoine was a nice looking young man with curly blond hair and brown eyes that seemed to smile at you when you greeted him. He was always smiling one way or another. People simply grew fond of him. He had a way of wanting people. Yes, wanting. You know what I mean by that. You should know by now. What I liked about him is that he did not leave me behind. He somehow carried me with him either in his pouch that he carried around or in his large pocket. He liked to show me to kids and even to some grown-ups. Yes, some people smiled seeing a grown man carrying a doll. He told people that I was une poupée qui apporte le bonheur/ a doll that brought happiness. Everyone of them wanted to touch me and some wanted to handle me and even bring me home with them. You see, they were poor people who had practically nothing and certainly did not taste le bonheur in their meager lives. I felt sorry for them especially the children who went begging for coins and even cigarettes. Antoine used to dig into his pockets and find some coins that he gave away but he did not have too much money on him. He was afraid of robbers and cheaters. He certainly was afraid of losing me in the crowds holding me tight in his right hand or putting his hand on me in his pocket. That's when I was afraid of choking or being squeezed too hard. He knew that and so he was very careful not to hurt me. He was indeed a kind and beautiful person. I liked him, no I loved him. I knew he was definitely a wanting person, that's why. Wanting attracts love.

I was kind of scared when Antoine and I walked in the ghettos or poor areas because I could see as Antoine did, all the poverty around us, the open garbage, the dirty muddy lanes as well as the dusty ones with all kinds of junk that people threw away, the crumbling porches, the not too clean laundry on the lines, and the way people lived. Many of the old people remembered the hard-line Papa Doc as well as his son, Baby Doc who took the money that other countries gave them, like he United States, and squandered it on themselves. That's besides the cruelty they inflicted on the citizenry. The poor people could not defend themselves, I was told, so they felt helpless and unwanted. That in itself is terrible, I think. How can a leader be so cruel, greedy and especially unwanting of the very people they govern? Their own people at that. Didn't the leaders of the other countries see that. I mean all the cruel things these so-called leaders did and how they ont gaspillé l'argent destiné au peuple de Haiti/ squandered all the money destined for the people of Haiti. That's how Antoine put it and I told him I agreed with him. It's truly a terrible situation in Haiti. By the way, there was so much wanting between Antoine and me(I call it love) that the communication line was well established between us, if you want to know.

Antoine and I went to visit a missionary one day. He was an Oblate of Mary the Immaculate and he had been serving the spiritual needs of the people here for over thirty years, he told Antoine. He came from Maine but his training was done in Massachusetts. He had volunteered to become a missionary and his superiors had sent him to Haiti because he spoke French and people spoke French in Haiti as well as creole. His name was Father Bolduc. He seemed to be a nice man, a wanting/wanted man. People loved him and his kind and sweet disposition. I like people like that. Father told Antoine that the people he served were poor and many of them destitute. They had nothing and wished for nothing except enough food for every day for themselves and their children. When Antoine showed me, the doll, to the children who had come surrounding the priest, their friend, all of them wanted to hold me. I was the doll they never had, you see and they were told that I brought happiness. "Oui, oui, je la veux, je la veux"/ I want her, I want her, they shouted. I was so glad. They wanted me, me a doll in a faraway country. A country so poor that the entire world had pity on it and its people, but did very little to reduce its pain and suffering. I found that terible." C'est terrible sinon horrible", said Antoine to Father Bolduc. The good priest simply nodded his head and said nothing except to mumble something like "Oui, c'est horrible si on encourage le démon dans sa destruction de l'âme de ces pauvres affamés de bonté et de divine grâce"/it's horrible if we encourage the devil in his destruction of these poor souls famished for goodness and divine grace. Antoine cast his watery eyes on the children surrounding us and uttered a muffled, oui.

    Father Bolduc developed a relationship with Antoine that bloomed and extended Antoine's connection with the people so that Antoine could easily touch the lives of many by speaking to them and begging them to tell their stories. He learned a lot from them. For example, he learned that the government offered practically no support to these people who were suffering from lack of food, clean water, poor health and many other problems. Antoine spoke to this woman who had nine children whose husband was without work and out of the nine children seven had some kind of illness. She could not see a doctor to take care of them. She had to beg and beg people to help her. The pharmacies refused to give her medication needed for those children for she had no prescriptions and no money. What to do? She appealed to Father Bolduc who was able to give her some money that he had gotten from home in the U.S. That helped a bit, but it wasn't enough. Father Bolduc ran around the parish solliciting funds for this lady.
He did that during his off-hours when he wasn't busy with parish tasks. He told Antoine that he was not able to get too much sleep and that he worried constantly about women like her and their families. Antoine often found Father Bolduc in the small chapel praying and even praying while shedding tears. That's how much he cared for his people and their problems. The good Father even went without food sometimes in order to provide funds and some meals to those who were in dire need of something just for survival sake. Antoine would often invite me to talk to him, some said that he talked to himself, but he was indeed communicating with me. He wanted to release his pent up emotions and wanted me, at times, to pray with him just so he could say he was doing something for these poor poor people he got to know. I told him that he had become a missionary just like Father Bolduc.

    Antoine in some way adopted a young boy who had lost his mother and whose father became an alcoholic. The poor lad ran away and sought shelter in some abandoned hut near the rectory. His name was André. André was about seven years old. He had no one to take care of him, no relatives, no friends, no one. That was so sad. Antoine felt sorry for the boy. He invited André to come and live with us in our house. It was small but decent. The boy did some chores for Antoine and Antoine rewarded him with food and some money. André loved to hear stories that Antoine told him at night before going to bed. The boy did not have a bed but an old mattress thrown on the kitchen floor for him. Antoine did not have an extra bed and he did not want to share his bed with the boy so that people would believe that he was abusing the boy in any way. He was simply giving shelter and food to André. The poor boy was so happy and really felt wanted. That was the key to his immediate happiness. I know how that feels.

Well, this woman came up to our place one day and introduced herself as André's cousin. She spoke creole and told Antoine that she was going to take care of the boy and Antoine by cleaning and preparing food for them. Antoine wondered where this woman was coming from. What did she want and why. It turned out that she had heard about me, the doll of happiness/la poupée de bonheur and she wanted desperately to get to me and possess me for she had heard that I brought happiness to the one who possesses me. How did she get to know this? I suppose from someone who had seen me and my sticker. Sometimes Antoine let some people handle me and take me in their hands. He allowed that sometimes. I liked it and I didn't like it. I did not want to be kidnapped and probably be sold to the highest bidder or something. I wanted to remain in Antoine's possession. He was my wanted/wanting friend and the one I had been confided to by Marianne.

Well, even though Antoine did not want her around, she stuck to us like an unwanted clam or a barnacle and we could not get rid of her. Sure, she did some cleaning and tried to cook some creole meal for us like the soupe joumou/ squash soup, but Antoine refused her offer. Besides, Antoine did not like squash and even pumpkin although André would eat anything. The lady whose name was Boulou, what a funny name, was into dolls, voudoo dolls, we later found out. She just did not want to leave. She kept uttering creole phrases like a pita/ see you later, tout moun, se moun/ everyone matters, and dézolé/ sorry. The boy translated for Antoine. You see creole means that its roots are African. That's all I know.

One day when Antoine was looking for Father Bolduc in the neighborhood, Boulou found me in Antoine's room. Antoine had left me behind thinking I would be safe. Well, the old hag found me and grabbed me. She grabbed me so tight that it really frightened me. André saw what she was doing and told her to leave me alone. She slapped him and made him cry. Then she told him that if he told Antoine about it she would come and grab him and take him away. She threatened him by telling him that she would use voudoo magic and turn him over to the devil. I could see that the poor boy was terribly frightened of her. He ran outdoors and left me with her holding me in her grubby hands. I wish I could have screamed but I couldn't. Help! Au secours! I would have shouted, but I couldn't. I felt so useless in my abilities as a doll. Useless and helpless. Of course, I was wanted but for the wrong reasons, I tell you.

So, the lady or rather the old hag Boulou wrapped me in a pillow case and brought me home with her. I was kidnapped! Once there wherever there was, I lay there in the pillow case for several hours unable to move my arms nor my legs. They were moveable after all. Then someone came in and started talking in creole that I did not understand. Besides I had no communication line with the old hag. I did not want any. All I wanted was my Antoine. Would he ever find me? What was going to happen to me? Was I lost forever? Would anyone rescue me? were all questions I had in my consciousness. I closed my eyes and went to sleep.

The following morning, I thought I heard a familiar voice. It was that of Father Bolduc who was asking the kidnapper lady questions about her activities and her thefts. Apparently, Boulou was a thief besides being a kidnapper of dolls like me. All that I could make out from their talking was the fact that Boulou had promised the priest to behave more like a Christian and less with voudooism. Now she was being accused by several people of playing with fire, sticking needles in her voudoo dolls and burning some of them in the local cemetery where the dead lay and where the devil prowled through the night waiting to catch some of the souls that had been seen ghostly floating in the night air. That's what people said. Boulou apparently was a curse to ordinary people who were terribly afraid of someone like Boulou dealing with the devil. Some were deadly afraid of her not wanting to be replicated as a voudoo doll with pins stuck here and there and then cursed for all eternity by a bonfire lit by the devil's hell fire. So they said. I did not know anything about voudoo in Haiti and I was longing to go home, back to France with Marianne. She was my so-called permanent agent and holder. For how long? I did not know. All I knew was that Haiti was not a place for me. I kept saying over and over, "Get me out of here. Out of this damn pillow case." It was stifling and I felt abducted by an old hag who probably wanted either to sell me or waiting for me to bring her happiness. No way, was I going to bring her happiness. First of all she did not deserve it and then she was not the one to duly possess me. I only bring happiness to someone who is pure in thought and virtuous in action. I mean not someone who deals with evil and Satan the devil. That's all wrong. Talk about wanting and wanted, I certainly did not want that at all. "Help! Au secours!"

Finally help did come since Father Bolduc suspected that Boulou had stolen me and had told Antoine about it. Antoine came into Boulou's house which was a kind of half demolished shack and he warned Boulou that he was going to have her arrested for stealing. At first, she denied having taken me but seeing the anger in Antoine's eyes and hearing it in his voice, she relented and went to get me in the pillow case. When she handed it over to him she said, "Dézolé"/I'm sorry. The devil made me do it." Father Bolduc told Antoine later on that Boulou was incited by her creole nature and was really a poor woman living alone who was grappling with her African roots and heritage like so many in Haiti. Antoine felt sorry for her and he decided to forgive her and even gave her some money to buy honest food. I remember she knelt down in front of him and kissed his hand. She was crying. Father Bolduc told Antoine that she was seeking pardon from him just like she did at confession with him. However, he told Antoine that Boulou soon forgets her sins and is ready to commit some more witthout fully knowing what she was doing or wanting to do. "She's a very poor woman in things and in her mind," Father said to Antoine. "God forgives her, but she is warned through me not to deal with the devil and his voudoo tricks for she will damn herself doing so. But she is weak and practically mindless at times and so I try to be compassionate with her." "I understand," said Antoine to him. We never saw Boulou again. Someone said that she was hiding in the woods afraid of the devil she had tried to cast aside but never could. She was cursed for life, some people said. They said that she was neither wanted by God nor the devil, Satan. Poor poor thing, poor creature of God, I thought. After all, she was created by him. That's truly a very sad thing for any human being. That's really not being wanted at all.

Antoine callled Marianne and told her he was ready to bring me back to France and give the happiness doll, that's me, back. He did not want to interfere with the true plight of la poupée de bonheur. That was to hand me over to the one who will possess me for good. Antoine was returning to France to be a speaker at a Francophone conference in Honfleur. He told me that this was the locale where Samuel de Champlain had left to go and explore the territory that was known as la Nouvelle-France. That some day it would be known as Canada and le Québec. Champlain was a very important historical figure and Antoine was going to speak about his influence on the Francophone heritage in Quebec and New England. I said to myself, I've been there. I'm part of history now. Well, somehow. You see I may be just a doll but I've learned things, things that are important.

In a way, I was glad we were leaving Haiti. I found the people there very kind in their own way but the climate of violence, distrust and political greed was not to my liking. I'm sure it wasn't in Antoine's either. So we left after we said goodbye to Father Bolduc, the dedicated Oblate missionary who really cared for his parishioners, people of simplicity and poverty in my estimation. Will they ever be able to get out of their misery, I asked myself. I sure hope so. They're really not wanted by their government and that's sad, cruel and discouraging. Their leader must give courage back to his people. After all, they are the very soul of Haiti. How can a nation survive without the courage of people being wanted and truly loved as human beings. Haitians are not robots nor are they men and women to be treated as criminals or beings worthy of rejection and be discarded like an old raggedy doll ready for the garbage heap. Poverty of means and the frowning of human dignity are, after all, not assets nor are they meant for people whoever they are and wherever they live. I don't know what the answer is. I'm just a doll.

Antoine and I arrived in Paris on a beautiful summer's day in July just as the French were preparing to celebrate Bastille Day, le 14 juillet. Celebration was in the air. People sat in cafés and drank wine while they chatted with friends and tourists who happened to pass by and ask directions to the Eiffel Tower or to the Louvre. One Frenchman pointed to the Eiffel Tower indicating it was self evident.

No need for directions, Monsieur. Marianne met us near the Place de la Concorde. It's the largest square in Paris, Marianne told Antoine. From there she brought us to the Tuileries Garden where Marianne and Antoine had a long chat about our stay in Haiti. I felt so very comfortable there lying alongside Marianne and Antoine on the bench. She told him that she regretted sending the two of us to Haiti, but she wanted for us, especially me, to get to know deep down the poor people and their misery of being used as slaves practically by their leaders. I felt sad about them but I didn't want to get involved with the politics of the land. What could I do? I was simply a doll. Marianne heard through our communication line what I felt and gave me to understand that she was trying to sensitize me to the situation in Haiti. That if I really cared for the people there I would take into consideration their full situation and their political plight. She said that she did not think I should get involved directly with politics but that I should keep in mind the full dilemma of the people there, the dilemma of not doing anything and being passive or consider revolution which is a very thorny and messy thing to do. I told Marianne that I understrood where she was coming from. But, I told her, I'm just a doll. What do you expect me to do? "Apprends"/learn, she said.

Marianne then brought us to the Orangerie Museum because Antoine wanted to see, once more, the eight paintings of the Monet series, "The Water Lillies", les nénuphars. That's how they call water lilies. I love that term since it's so poetic and if you say it out loud it rings with delight just like a tuba. Am I crazy or what? There was a large round seat in the middle of the huge circular room and that's where Marianne put me while she and Antoine went around the enormous circular display of the Water Lillies paintings. I could hear Antoine sighing and exclaiming oh's and ah's while standing before one of the Impressionist paintings. "They're so beautiful these immortal paintings, ces nénuphars de gloire et de douces couleurs dans une eau tranquille et sereine"/ these water lillies of glory and of sweet colors in a tranquil and serene water, he said. I saw Marianne nodding her head . Antoine must have revered these paintings with awe since I could hear him sigh and utter sincere and pleasant comments about the fascinating paintings. "Look at this one how the water lillies seem to float in a dream. They are simply marvelous and so real to the eye. I feel that I'm with Monet in Giverny and looking deeply in the waters where he was painting these exquisite flowers. They are simply exquisite. I saw them once. I took photos of them but my photos do not compare with these striking paintings. I simply love them since I feel that I'm enjoying a dream, a dream of sensuality and artistic joy. Mmmm, Marianne let's stay here and share the dream, the dream of contentment and pleasurable feelings. Le rêve d'un bonheur exquis"/ the dream of an exquisite happiness. Marianne then told Antoine they had to move on, want to or not. However, we stayed there practically glued to these paintings with me lying there on soft cushions listening to the sounds of delight and artistic pleasure. Humans are so lucky to have such treasures of art at their disposal. I thought, "Am I the result of art or the work of an ordinary maker of dolls who could care less about art?" What is art anyway? I cannot define it but I do realize that certain human beings can because they have acquired the sensitivity and true realization of art. Art is the reproduction of tangible beauty in life, I thought. Am I right or am I wrong? From the Orangerie Museum, we went outside on the vast terrace where were exhibited some sculptures. I didn't care where I was going as long as I was with my two best friends. Yes, I had grown very fond of Antoine. Had I been a human girl, I would have taken Antoine as my boyfriend, if he would have me. I know I would have wanted him. You know what I mean, don't you? As for Marianne, you can see that I have been very fond of her from the beginning of our relationship. She wants me and I want her. Two wanted creatures of time and circumstance.

  As the two of them were walking, they noticed Rodin's famous sculpture of "The Kiss." Marianne held me up and told me to open my eyes to take a good look at this beautiful large sculpture of a man and a woman kissing. "Wow!" I uttered, "that's so good and so well done. Why did Rodin sculpt this?" I asked her. Marianne began to tell me all about it when Antoine said, "Les poupées ne s'embrassent pas"/dolls don't kiss. "Mais, oui, elles s'embrassent avec le coeur"/they kiss with the heart, she told him. Oh, I totally agreed with her. Then she began telling the story behind the sculpture, "The Kiss." "You see, Rodin got the inspiration from Dante's eternal epic of the Divine Comedy in which we find the tale of Paolo and Francesca who are slain by the husband when he discovers them having their first kiss. They are condemned to wander eternally through Hell, Dante tells us. Isn't that a tender and tragic story?" I thought so but Antoine differed from me. He thought that the husband should have been sent to jail and the lovers each one sent to spend the rest of their lives in a monastery somewhere. Marianne asked him why, and he told her that he was going to tell her later when they would have dinner. She looked at him with a dimpled smile and a glint in her eye. Then we started to walk away. "Wait, I forgot I had Founie in my pocket, poor thing, she must be choking or having a hard time seeing things," said Marianne. "Well, take her out of there. Tu brises son bonheur"/ you're breaking her happiness, said Antoine. No one breaks my happiness. No one. It's mine and mine to give. La poupée qui apporte le bonheur/the doll that brings happiness. That's who I am. That's what makes me invulnerable at all instances of human neglect or forgetfulness. So, let's move on, dear friends of mine. Move on to the glamor of wanting and being wanted. You see, I cannot help myself, readers. C'est plus fort que moi/it's stronger than me. Me, a doll of value to those who believe in dreams and promises put on stickers. Oh, there should be more stickers like mine put on every human being who shares the dream. It's not an illusion. It's a dream. Dreams are real, folks. They are real. I closed my eyes so that I could see dreamland from afar. Dreamland, la-la land and whatever you may want to call it. It's real. Then I heard Marianne say to Antoine, "Sors de ton rêve, Antoine, regarde là-bas c'est Paris en lumière resplendissante"/get out of you dream, look over there at Paris resplendant in light. I guess Antoine was walking not noticing things as if he was sleep-walking and Marianne had to wake him up. She woke me up too for I had my eyes closed as if nothing mattered but the fact of being carried in Antoine's magical pocket. It was as if he was carrying me to the stars. Hey, I'm dreaming now. Think of it Marianne, Antoine and I are walking in Paris the most beautiful city in the entire world! C'est une cité resplendissante de rêves et de poésie " it's a city gleaming with dreams and poetry.

I have to wake up if I'm going to continue telling my story. The doll with imaginary dreams, but also with a keen eye for real things. You see, I'm not stupid. I know how to see things and relate them to you readers. I may be just a doll but I'm an extraordinary doll. Wouldn't you say so?

Marianne, Antoine and I went to a lovely café on the Boulevard Montparnasse. They talked about the literary people who went there to eat and drink such as Ernest Hemingway and others. The café or rather the restaurant is known as "La Closerie des Lilas" and it serves delightful seafood and is well-known for its huîtres/oysters. Antoine and Marianne took a Dégustation seafood platter. It looked very good but, of course, I have no taste for food. I was glad they were enjoying the selection. My food is enjoying the pleasures of a doll's life with the little extras such as communicating with some humans and finding out what motivates them to do what they are doing like traveling and spending time talking to one another. Yes, humans, some humans, or I should say many human beings love to talk. Talk, talk, talk, that's all they do. Whew, that's tiring, I should think. I find that a lot of it is useless talk. It's chatter. I'm glad that both Marianne and Antoine do not chatter uselessly. They talk, yes, but they do not talk uselessly. What they say usually matters and I don't have to listen to some ridiculous chatter with them. I learn from them. I love to learn what they think about people and their infinite capabilities to appreciate what is good in life such as art, good food and wanting and being wanted. That, I really like. You know why. I'm a doll. I like what I like and what's important. If it's not important, well I just let it pass by or neglect the so-called un-importance of it such as the chatterbox syndrome that negates the seriouness of living and coping. Some learn to cope with things and people while others do not. They struggle and find utter frustration or disgust. It's terrible. As a doll, I cope with almost everything, well, almost. It's hard for me to try and cope with unwanting people who are never satisfied with anything or anyone. What do you want? I would ask them. But of course, they would answer, I don't know. Awh, gawd! Bless them little idiots. Oops, sorry, that slipped out. Dolls are not supposed to dislike anything or anyone. We're not made that way. I think that's good. I must stop chatter-think that way. That's not my destiny as a man-made thing. Yes, I'm a thing with extraordinary features, that's all. Oh, stop it, I tell myself. Stop the chatter. Chatter is talk for nothing. I know that. You don't have to tell me. I'm a doll that must not go beyond the capacities of doll-being. Stop it, I tell myself, stop saying things that some people will not fully understand. I know but some people do and that's all that matters to me. I'm a doll and I like being a doll. That's me, Founie. What a curious name, don't you think? Founie, Founie, a name that links the doll-world with the people-world. Don't you think that's funny? It's not funny, I tell myself. It's hilariously strange. That's all. Enough of this. That's enough or else people will stop wanting to listen to my story. After all, that's my reason for being here.

Je dois rester calme et sans paroles inutiles/ I must remain calm and without useless words. Oui, messieurs, mesdames, à votre service/at your service. Founie aime plaire/loves to please. Shut up, Founie, I tell myself and I go back to Antoine's large deep pocket. Marianne puts me there before walking away from Boulevard Montparnasse. She looks back at the restaurant, smiles a weary smile, lifts up her head towards the sky and utters "Aurevoir, chère maison de dégustation, aurevoir aux huîtres si délicieuses d'autrefois au bord de la mer où nous dégustions les fruits de mer en famille. On se donnait le plaisir de goûter le soleil et sa chaleur ainsi que les merveilleuses délices qu'offrait la mer." /so long, dear house of tasting delicacies, so long the delights of partaking oysters seaside where seafood family-style was enjoyed. We gave ourselves the pleasure of tasting the warmth of the sun as well as the marvelous delights that the sea offered us. Oh yes, one could have seen and tasted the joys of yesteryear when the family got together and we forgot the pains of dreariness and wanting to belong to someone somewhere. All of that disappeared with one whiff of the sea air."

I did not have a family like Marianne had nor did I crave for one, but I did relish the friendship that I built with these two friends. It was somewhat of a strange friendship, a doll and its owners, or should I say confidants, but it became a wanting friendship, if you know what I mean. Oh, sure you do, for I have said it so many times before. You're not stupid. You're a sharp reader and you must have learned things by now. I mean the things I have been talking about and what you have read so far. You're not stupid, I'm not stupid, so who is? No one. No one is stupid. Only those who choose to be stupid are. It's that simple in doll-land. I don't know about human-land. I would rather not think about it. Besides, Forest Gump's mother used to tell him, "Stupid is as stupid does." Well, that's a line to remember, don't you think? I like Forest Gump. Don't you think he's a likeable guy? His mother loves him and she thinks he's got some talent for something. He's not stupid, just a bit simple-minded, that's all. Simple-minded with a kind and wanting heart. I say blessed those who have a wanting heart. They are blessed by the good spirit, the spirit that lives in all souls. All human beings have souls. That's what Father Bolduc used to say to his brebis/his sheep as he called them. I didn't think his parishioners were sheep. They were not animals. But I took it that he meant they were his loved ones , like a sheepherder who loves his sheep. I prefer the lambs to the full-grown sheep myself. They're so cute and cuddly. They get your affection right away as soon as you see one standing there or sitting in the grass sweetly bleating. Or is it lying down or even crouching? You tell me. I'm just a doll.

Marianne invited Antoine to her house on rue de Chevreuse or rather it was an apartment in the center of Paris, I think. She wanted to talk about his visit to Haiti. She told him that she thought it was a good idea on her part to take me there and show me to the children and at the same time get acquainted with the culture. She was sorry about the incident with Boulou and her stealing me. She realized, she told him, that I had to be protected at all times. She confessed to me later that she had thought of sending me to Vietnam where there had been the French influence at one time or another but then she realized that it would have been dangerously close to terrorism if I went there. I asked her what terrorism was and she told me that I did not want to hear about it. I told her that I was open to anything and that I needed to know things and movements and stuff like that. She then warned me about stuff like that since stuff does not teach one anything good. It teaches bad things and that it was in my interest not to find out about bad stuff. I told her that I did not want to remain ignorant about important things and that it was better to know about stuff than to avoid learning about it. So she realized that I made sense and started to tell me about terrorism. When she got done, I cringed a bit and worried that terrorism would eventually spread throughout the world and that I would be caught in it. Terrorism is a terrible thing because it uses violence to unleash fear and fear produces anxiety and horrible feelings of being unsafe and in danger most of the time. She told me that terror started with the French Revolution when it seemed that all hell had broken loose and Robespierre began killing innocent people for nothing. "Who's Robespierre?" I asked her. "You don't really want to know," she said. "Alright if you say so, I'm just a doll." So, I was glad that she had not sent me to Vietnam where I could have encountred terror. I told myself that I had had enough terror with Boulou and her tactics of fear and theft. She was quite the gal that one. She had used me to get what she wanted, whatever that was. That was not a good wanting in my book. No 'Mam.

Following my stay in Paris with Marianne (Antoine had left to go home in Quebec) I was sent to another place where they spoke French and where Marianne had another connection. This time it was a woman who had fire in her eyes and in her heart. She was called "la gitane enflammée de Saintes-Maries de la mer"the gypsy of fire. I was being sent to the very southern tip of France where Gypsies congregate once a year to celebrate their favorite saint, Sara la Kali. That would be very interesting, I told myself. Une poupée qui apporte le bonheur aux gitans/ a doll that brings happiness to the Gypsies. Well bring on the fun and the celebration, I told Marianne. She smiled and kissed me on the head right on my faded bonnet. "Nous partons demain matin"/we're leaving tomorrow morning, she said.

We left early in the morning of a March day when the sun was barely on the horizon. Marianne wanted to take an early train at la Gare du Sud. She already had made reservations and was waiting for the taxi to bring her there. She had me in her large leather bag that she loved when she travels. The taxi driver asked her if she was alone travelling and she answered,

---Non, monsieur, j'ai mon amie avec moi/ no, I have my friend with me.
----Mais, je ne la vois pas/ but I don't see her, her told her.
---Mon amie est dans mon sac à main/my friend is in my handbag.
---Mon Dieu, ce n'est pas possible!/it's not possible, he told her.
---C'est une poupée/it's a doll.
The taxi driver was all startled.
---Une jeune demoiselle comme vous,, grandette et bien accomplie comme vous, vous jouez avec des poupées?/ a grown woman like you, you play with dolls?

Marianne answered by saying,
---Pourquoi pas, Monsieur? Tout le monde a besoin d'une poupée pour les désennuyer, même les hommes/ everyone needs a doll to relieve them of boredom, even men.
---Pas moi, je vous l'assure. Pas moi, certainement pas moi. Mademoiselle, je suis un homme pas un efféminé ni une poule mouillée/ not me, I assure you. certainly not me. I'm a man not a sissy nor a coward.
---Avez-vous peur de regarder ma poupée? Y jeter un coup d'oeil

seulement? Si oui, vous êtes une poule mouillée./ are you afraid of looking at my doll? Only catching a glance at her?If it's yes them you're a coward.

---Je ne suis pas un peureux ni une poule mouillée. Montrez-la-moi votre poupée/ I'm not afraid nor am I a coward. Show me you doll.
Marianne took me out of her bag and showed me to the taxi driver who was a big and tall man with a huge mustache.I opened my eyes wider to notice that he looked squeamish. Was he afraid of handling a doll, I wondered.

---Prenez-la dans votre main. Elle ne mord personne. Elle est douce comme un petit mouton/Take her in your hands. She bites no one. She's as sweet as a lamb.

---Mais elle est laide votre poupée. C'est une poupée de marché aux puces. J'en ai vue de ces rejets./but she's ugly your doll. It's a flea market doll. I've seen some like that, they're rejects.
I trembled inside of me. I did not want to be handled by a man like that, burly, ugly himself and an unwanting person. No , no way did I want him to touch me.

----Elle n'est pas laide, ma poupée, ni est-elle méchante. C'est une poupée qui apporte le bonheur à ceux et celles qui la possèdent. Voyez son étiquette ici sur sa blouse/She's not ugly, my doll, nor is she bad. It's a doll that brings happiness to those who possess her. Here's her sticker on her blouse, look at it.

---Ça alors, laissez-moi la prendre. Je la prendrai gentillement/ then let me take her. I'll handle her gently.

I must tell you I still did not trust him. He was not the trustworthy kind. I tried to tell Marianne that I did not want him to touch me but she did not fulfull my request. Later on, she told me that she wanted me to get used to unsavory characters and be kind to them. I tried, you can rest assured. I really tried but I did not like it. People, my readers, in the future please do not let big burly unwanting fellows get a hold of me. I only want wanting people to touch me. Okay?

Well, he did hold me in his right hand and started looking at my sticker. He read it and gave me back to Marianne.

---Est-ce que je peux l'avoir ta poupée? can I have you doll
---Pourquoi/why?

----Parce qu'elle m'apporterait le bonheur que j'ai tant cherché. Pourtant je le mérite/because she would bring me the happiness I've been looking for...for such a long time. Yet, I deserve it.

---Si vous le méritez vous l'aurai, mais ma poupée n'est pas à donner. Elle m'appartient et c'est tout/ If you deserve it you will get it but my doll is mine and it's not to give away and that's all.

----Je la donnerais à ma petite fille qui souffre de l'ennui et du rejet. Elle n'a que quatre ans. Sa maman est malade et elle ne peut pas lui offrir de cadeaux/ I would give it to my little girl who suffers from boredom and rejection. She's only four years old. Her mother is sick and she cannot offer her any gifts.

I tried to tell Marianne that the little girl who suffers from rejection might be the one who is destined to possess me as the sticker says. Marianne did not believe so, because she answered me in her unmistakable vibes that she used with me that the man was lying. He was making things up, she said. How did she know? Well she read his license and the guy was not married."Son permis le contredit"/ his permit or license contradicts him. Well, don't give me away, I told her. Put me back in your bag where I belong. Some people will do anything to possess me. Not necessarily me but the happiness I bring. I repeat, happiness is earned, not simply given away like that. I know my destiny and the reason behind my journey as a doll, a carrier of good fortune. That's all I have to say.

Marianne told the taxi driver whose name was Judas (yes, really, Judas) to get going since she was in a hurry to get to the train station. She didn't want to miss her train. "Let's get out of here and get rid of this man who is so strange and and a liar. I don't like people who tell lies. They're like ugly ducklings. I only like beautiful people who tell the truth. That's what makes them filled with beauty. Take the roses, for instance, they're nature's holders of truth and beauty. People like them and cultivate the. They even give them names. One doesn't bestow a name on an ugly sort of being, do you?" Marianne smiled and continued reading her book. We were now on the train in Marianne's seat. It was Le Petit Prince, a lovely story of a little boy-prince from outerspace who cares very much for his rose. Read it some day. I was told the story by another acquaintance of mine years ago. You see, I've been around for quite sometimes.

    While Marianne was reading, I was comfortably sleeping in her large bag on top of her make-up kit with a soft velvety cover. I could smell her perfume and her deodorant. Marianne is a clean and well-ordered little lady. She likes things to be well arranged and duly used without too much bother. She adjusted my blouse and pants so that they fitted better on me and I looked well trimmed and proper. That was her words, "propre et bien attelée. She had gotten that word from her visit to Quebec. Québécois do not always use Parisian words; they use some of theirs sometimes like attelé which comes from dressing a horse or something. She did not like my old faded bonnet but that's all I had and I wasn't going to change it for something else. People have to accept me the way I am, I told her. What could she do? I was a flea market doll and I was going to stay that way. It didn't matter how I looked or where I came from, I was Founie the doll with a happiness sticker and I was on a journey that was meant to be a wanted/wanting journey , and not to forget a giving away journey. You know what I mean, don't you? Good, I hate repeating things.

I must not forget something and that's the name of the one who sent me and why. Most people ask me about it and they deserve an answer. The name of the person who sent me here. Actually it wasn't a person, it was an angel. Yes, an angel from up above. It was a she, not a girl and not a woman. A she angel. Her name was Angelica. You know, Angel, Angelica. Not the one from EWTN. She's somewhere floating in the beyond awaiting her mission. She was a good talker for sure. People liked her. Why she could talk you ears off. That's how good she was. It was another creature who was very good at giving instructions to dolls, someone like me. She's the one who probably put that sticker on me. I don't know. Anyhow, that man in Tuscany duplicated it and he and Simone put them on dolls they purchased and then sold or profit. Angelica did not want to make profit on me but all she wanted was to find the right human being who could possess me in a true and honest way. That is, truly want me and care if I'm given a good home or not, a home where there is love and devotion to genuine caring for dolls like me. That was her mission, you see, and it was all dedicated to dolls. After all, dolls don't have guardian angels so they need someone or something to take care and manage them. She did not realize that I was going to end up in a flea market though. But that's towards the end of my story, readers. Just wait. It will be worthwhile, I guarantee you.

My story, my story, where was I? Oh, yes, Marianne, my keeper, and I we're going to the south of France to a place called Saintes-Maries de la Mer. That's quite a name, Marys of the sea. The sea, the sea, we're going to the sea! Good Lord whoever you are, we're going to the sea. I can't believe it. I always wanted to go to the sea and take a long look at the bright and deep waters where fish swim, whales jump, porpoises and seals enjoy the fun they get from frolicking in the waters, and, yes, all the boats that sail those waters and capture plentiful sea creatures that provide food for people who might go hungry if they did not benefit from fishermen's catches. I met a fisherman once but that's another story. I have many stories to tell. You see, I'm a doll who brings happiness but I'm also a good storyteller. I met this man once, a writer and a published author, who kept saying and believing that human beings are fundamentally stotytellers. It goes back to the days of creation, he said. The first stories were cast in myth, he said.

Again, I tell you that's another episode and I'm not ready to say anything about it. One story at a time, one episode at a time. That's my train of thought and my venture in my doll's life. Understand?

Saintes-Maries-de-la-Mer is a fisherman's delight and un lieu sacré de pèlerinage pour les gitans"/a sacred place of pilgimages for the Gypsies, as Marianne put it. She was so happy to be back here. She had been to Saintes-Maries some time ago but had not returned. This was a pure delight for her since she knew several people who lived here. "Smell the freshness of the sea air and the cooking and baking of Meditarranean cuisine" she said. But I told her I couldn't fully smell. I told her that I was limited in my smelling. Sure, I have a nose but it's not a human nose. Humans are lucky. They can smell things like cooking, the smell of fresh fish and oh, the perfume of flowers. Remember humans, noses are very important so keep them clean and don't let smoke get in the way like cigarette smoke. Bad for you, I'm sure. Worse, is the terrible impure unclean air when fossil fuel spews its dirt in the air and factories do the same thing. Someday the earth will spew it right back and the entire atmosphere will feel its unwanted stench and filth. What are you talking about? is the line that I get when I say such things. Well, it's true and don't you forget it. But, I'm just a doll. Nobody ever believes me. Why should they? Well, they should believe somebody somewhere who clamors about it. Clamor, yes clamor means shouts from the rooftops and mountain tops, Hey, everybody wake up and live a pure and clean air life. Now that I have said my piece, let's return to my story and Saintes-Maries-de-la-Mer. Oh, this place is so clean and bright. It's no wonder the Gypsies love it.

    Marianne took me to the church where the Gypsies's saint is located. Yes, they have their own saint and she is called Sara la Kali. Marianne says that they venerate her as their queen. She's a dark or black saint, she wears a crown and she is loaded with brightly colored veils, cloaks and all kinds of rich garments that the Gypsies have put on her. To me she's a giant doll. "Une poupée de richesse et de charme africain"/A doll of riches and of African charm, I told Marianne. And she replied, "Ce n'est pas une poupée mais une glorieuse statue d'une sainte reconnue pour sa valeur et son héritage de Romani"/It's not a doll but a glorious statue of a saint recognized for her value and Romani heritage. "But I see her as a huge black doll standing there",I said. "Don't go telling that to the Gypsies," she said to me. "Why not?" I said. "Because a doll is a doll and a statue is a representation of someone who is venerable. One does not venerate a doll. However, Sara la Kali is the Black Madonna that is the object of veneration honored powerfully by the Gypsies since it represents one of the important facets of being a Gypsy. She is the Queen, the Madonna and the great spirit of the Gypsies that gathers them into the folds of her brightly colored veils when a Gypsy comes to venerate Sara la Kali and kisses her feet . In one sense, she is sublime as the sacred feminine as well as humble like the humble Gypsy who lives life fully but with gusto. Then Marianne informed me that every year on May24-25 a great crowd of European Gypsies along with tourists and local residents gather to process the statue of Sainte Sara, Mary Salome and Mary Jacob into the waters and then back to their church. The Gypsies believe that's how they receive the blessings of these venerated saints. They consider them their very own. Gypsies are quite religious in their way. "Wow, can I go and be dipped in the waters of the sea?" I asked. Marianne replied, Non, ma chère poupée car tu es fragile et tu n'es pas sainte. Tu serais démolie vite dans l'eau et je te perdrais, probablement noyée."/No, my dear doll for you are fragile and not saintly. You would fall apart in the waters and I would lose you, probably drowned. I did not hesitate adding, "Oublions être plongée dans l'eau"/Let's forget about being plunged in the waters. Marianne started laughing and I tried to laugh too but only in my heart since I can't open my mouth to laugh like she does.

It was a small church with the two Marys in a boat sitting there next to a window. "Why are they sitting in a boat?" I asked. "Because they're the two holy women who stood at the foot of the cross and after Jesus's death they were carried away in a boat that landed on the beach that was part of what is now France." "Oh, that was surely a long time ago", I said. "Yes, a very long time ago." Then Marianne took me to the Camargue wetland where the pink flamingos and the wild horses can be seen. The flamingos are simply beautiful from afar. There were hundreds of them and it seemed like a pink moment of a dream. Then the wild horses trampling in the waters, white horses and guardians by their side energizing the wetland. It was all a dream to me. Marianne stood there saying nothing but I could tell she was transfixed by it all. Everything was so beautifully choreographed by nature, it seemed. Oh, yes, everything in wild nature is just, just......wonder shattering. You may wonder where I got all these magnificent words. From nature itself, I suppose. Yes, I do get inspired, you know. Words come into me like some magic. It has to be magic or the immersion into human life and its imitation. You see, I can imitate very well. Words and ideas simply come to me like breaths of living imitation. I simply suck them in my doll's being. I am a doll but an extraordinary one. I am made up of so many qualities that people don't really understand me and my gifts of being. I was made that way and besides I bring happiness to those who believe in me, partially and, of course, totally to the one who will possess me. I'm a DOLL! I'm a DOLL! I'm going nuts am I not.

Marianne grabbed me and that threw me out of my wondering and posturing. It really shook me up a bit. It seemed that I was in a crazy dream of wild horses, pink flamingos, splashing waters and wild Gypsies in celebration. Gypsies have life, full, passionate, and colorful life. I love them, them and their mysterious dark-complexioned Sara la Kali. I still say that she would make a great giant of a doll. Marianne insists she's not a doll but a statue. Well, she can say what she wants but I say Sara is a doll that brings excitement and crazy joy to the Gypsies. Not stupid joy but crazy joy that brings bubbles to the brain and the heart. Like champagne. Oh, I wish I could drink champagne but that's a human delight. Do you like champagne?

YOUNIE, THE FLEA MARKET DOLL

Enough of this babbling. I must get back to my story. Where was I? Oh, yes, on the banks of the wetland in Saintes-Maries-de-la-Mer in far south of France with Marianne who is dragging me around and showing me the wonders of the Gypsies. Marvelous people they are. They're so full of life and they sing loud and clear. I only wish I could sing with them when they begin to gather together and raise a storm at night by the fire. Especially when one of the men takes his violin and starts to play with such touching and heart-piercing fingers. I feel like I'm shivering all over. I'm lying right next to Marianne where she put me and I can feel her shivering, but her shivers are from the cold breezes of the night. She hurries to put a blanket around her shoulders. I can tell she's cold. I'm not. I'm always the same. I don't feel the cold nor the heat of the sun. I'm a doll, remember?

It was now the evening of May 25 and the great festival was ending. The caravans had started moving off. Marianne told me that most Gypsies are nomads and at no time do they know what tomorrow brings. I guess I'm a Gypsy for I never know where I'm going day to day. I follow the stars, I guess and I wander around until I fall into the hands of someone to whom I'm confided. Right now, no one possesses me. Marianne is as close as it gets but in truth, she does not possess me. I possess her. Yes, I do. She does what is best for me and my line of communication with her is full strength so that she does what I tell her in an indirect way. I possess her, you see. Yes, I do, believe me. It may not be direct and final, but it's my way of feeling that I possess her. Oh, well, think what you may but I possess her.

Well, we leave Saintes-Maries-de-la-Mer the next morning as well as the Gypsies who are going in many directions. Some will stop a while in Arles, but just for a few moments to see a friend or a relative who has stopped roaming and has settled there. Marianne reminds me that Arles was the place Van Gogh came when he first arrived in the plentiful sunshine of Provence. Oh yes, "Starry Starry Night" that great painting of his with stars whirling and the sky offering you the wildness of the soul at work creating dreams. Van Gogh who left the south to go back up north to die. From a bullet wound? What a great artist with a wild Gypsy-like streak in him, they say. Who says? The people who find him too wild or crazy for their taste, I suppose. Too bad the people in and around Arles and even at Saintes-Maries-de-la-Mer found him so strange they refused to even talk to him. Can you imagine that? Now thousands and thousands of people pay millions of dollars or whatever currency for one of his paintings when he couldn't even get a fair price for one when he was alive. Crazy! Did he really cut off his ear? Crazy! I'm a crazy doll.

We left Saintes-Maries-de-la-Mer late morning of the following day since Marianne wanted to rest and just lounge on the sands of the beach taking in the sun and the cool breezes that came off occasionally from the Mediterranean. I loved it lying there next to her, quiet, mellow, warm and still right there on the sand while she was gazing at the sky. I wished then that I was a human enjoying all senses and all openings of the creative mind. No, no I was a doll and I would stay that way. I then wondered what would happen to me once I had given the happiness promised to the one who would possess me. Would I become a dull doll? Haha, it's just a play on words, un calembour. Don't fret people. Don't let your senses be alarmed or your mind senseless. Haha, Got you.

Well, we did take the train back to Paris and I was thinking what was going to be our next adventure when Marianne told me that she was going to the opera. "The opera?" "Oui, l'Opéra de Paris, ma chère, l'opéra et sa musique et son drame. Je pense d'aller voir Les Contes d'Hoffman."/ opera and its music and drama. I'm thinking of going to see The Tales of Hoffman. "What's that?"

Well, we did go and see the Contes d'Hoffman and it was a delightful evening and somewhat of a strange opera, I think. I was sitting there on Marianne's lap. Some people did ask her what Marianne was doing with a doll at the opera. "Well, it's my Olympia," she told them. You see Olympia is the mechanical creation of a wizard, a doll that needs to be wound up now and then or else she or it just stops moving. So, she sings the "Doll Song" with very high notes. I loved it. A doll singing a doll song. How delightful. I wish I could sing, I would sing you my song, a song of happiness and gladness, glad to be with you and tell you my story. My story...oh, where was I?

My next part was with a young man who loved dolls and collected them. he was a kind of a strange but loving person who was not afraid of showing who he was and what he represented. He lived in Montreal and often visited Paris. He loved Paris. He told Marianne that some people called him queer while others called him gay. I like gay. It means joyful and happy, doesn't it? But why was he somewhat confused and even a bit sad. Because, Marianne said, he was, un homme aux hommes/ a man who loved men. "Is that all?" I said. "You don't understand." "What?" " A man who loves a man is strange to some people, queer, they say." "But strange, queer, what difference does that make?" "The difference being that a man should love a woman, make love to a woman, not another man." "Oh, that's it?" "Mmm." "But what's wrong with loving another man? Everybody should love everybody shouldn't they? "You don't understand." "I do. It's you who doesn't understand." "No, no, you are the one. Not me." "Alright if you say so. I'm just a doll, Une poupée mais une poupée qui apporte le bonheur et je suis donc gaie, gaieté, vive la gaieté!"/a doll but a doll that brings happiness and I'm thus gay, gaity, long live gaity. With that I was introduced to Michael Guay.

Michael Guay was an artist of daring perspetives. He did watercolors, oils, wood sculptures, and built houses with doors that reminded me of eyes opening and closing just like mine. A doll house! No, not a doll house but a gay house where people come and have a fun time. A house for partying you might say. You would be right but partying for fun and at the same time for sharing feelings and thoughts. He called them, meditation homes. People came and sat down to meditate about all kinds of things like money, jobs, travel, and needs of the soul. "Needs of the soul?" I asked. "Yes, needs of the soul, Founie. He was one of the very few who called me by my name. I loved him. He was a wanting/wanted person. I like that. You know why.

Among his works of art were knives with wood handles that he sculpted such as the human hand, the horse's head, the lion head with a blown-out mane, a heart cut in half for someone who is half-hearted, he said. I tell you, he was strange, queer. "Don't say that," Marianne told me. "Why not?" I answered. "Because, because you just don't say that about a gay person." "Why?"

"You don't understand." "Stop telling me that. Stop telling me that I don't understand...Alright, I don't understand. I'm a doll. Is that it?" "Non, non, non. ce n'est pas parce tu es une poupée mais une poupée qui ne peut pas tout comprendre dans le domaine du humain."/no, it's not because you are a doll but a doll that cannot understand everything in the human domain. I simply bowed my head in my limited understanding of human beings. Human beings are hard to understand sometimes. They go in circles and do not exercize all their talents as creative, thinking and mindful creatures. Sorry for that, humans. Grow up and take charge of everything that is being given to you. Like the power of love and compassion. Yes, love. That's more than a doll has. I can like but not love. Understanding is not always easy for dolls like me and I might add for some human beings too. Do you understand?

Well, Michael Guay was a good guy and we hit it off fast. Marianne introduced him to me at a party that he was giving in one of his houses on la rue Tizane. It was certainly a gay house with everybody having fun, drinking and eating all kinds of food. They really were having a good time. I could tell. Marianne was speaking to some guy that I did not know but that was alright, I was lying on top of some large fluffy towel on a wooden table where she had placed me. She did not abandon me. Don't go thinking she did. No, it was Michael who had put me there while he went around smiling and chatting with people. All of a sudden, someone picked me up and began looking under my blouse. I wanted to say "Don't do that. That's not very nice" but I could not get it out of me. We were not on communicatve line. So when he was done examining me, I opened my eyes and he started laughing. "Voilà une poupée qui semble en vie. Elle ouvre les yeux"/here's a doll who looks alive. It opens its eyes. Marianne rushed over and took me and put me in her large handbag. Ompf, I suffocated in there among all her belongings. I didn't want to be kept away from it all. I felt like a something being sent to jail, for what?

Before leaving the party, Marianne confided me, the doll that was in her handbag, she confided me to Michael. I was glad. Enough of that confinement though.

Enough of that stop-bothering-me affair. I wasn't bothering her. I was simply being examined by a pure stranger who did not understand dolls, I suppose. She felt bothered because she was sorry that she had left me behind with Michael who did not understand dolls like me who need to be protected somehow. Gawd, I didn't want to be kidnapped again. It's not fun. Was Marianne getting tired of me?

    Michael and I had fun, lots of fun. First he brought me to look at marionettes in a small theater off the beaten path, so to speak. It was far away from the hussle and bustle of Paris, not far from the Bois de Boulogne. It was a quiet place where one could hear the birds sing and the frogs croak in the pond. Michael had built a small house with a theater inside for those who wanted to put on plays and feature marionettes, if they wanted. I had never seen marionettes before. They're like dolls except they're tied to strings or wires and people make them jump, walk, do all kinds of tricks and pretend they are talking when it's the people's voice you hear. It's quite amusing. Very imaginative and creative, I would say. Entertaining too. Dolls that are strung up. Hmmmm. One of the marionettes got a hold of me by some communication device, I suppose. It wanted to get my attention. It was a clown, un Pierrot, with sad eyes and a tear on his cheek. " I want to get out of here" he tries to tell me as if I can do that. I like Pierrots but I can't get this one out of being a marionette. So, he jiggled, turned around and gave a big sigh that no one could see and hear. "Too bad," I said, " but I'm just a common ordinary doll who can't do extraordianry things like that," even though I was an extraordinary doll. But, I didn't want to tell him so. He would have bothered me all night long. Yes, we did spend the night there. We watched a play by a friend of Michael's. It was a play with two guys and the title was En Attendant Godot. It was a strange kind of a play, funny but sad. There are two main characters, Gogo and Didi and they talk and talk about waiting, waiting and loss of hope, I guess. I don't know why since there's always hope of some kind, hope that luck will come and, of course, happiness. Happiness is always in the cards, as they say. I know. Anyways who is that Godot? Why should they wait for him? Is he a nice guy? A happy guy? Who knows? It seemed absurd to me. "Yes", someone said, "it's the theater of the absurd." Later on, I was told that it was written by a French playwright, Samuel Beckett, who was born in Ireland and lived most of his life in Paris, was known for his skill as a writer and an activist. I wonder if he liked dolls. I would have given him one if I had known he liked them. I know of one doll that would have pleased him. The Cabbage Patch Kids made of cloth with a plastic face. Terribly popular at one time. Why Cabbage Patch Kids because I was told that the Irish love cabbage. Je ne sais pas si les Français aiment le chou/ I don't know if the French love cabbage. All I know is cabbage stinks when it's being cooked. Did you ever experience that. Whew! I never experienced it for I don't have the sense of smell, but I know it stinks. However, Cabbage Patch Kids did not stink. Dolls do not stink. Only if you put them in a garbage can with a lot of stinking stuff like old fish and rotten meat.

Michael was always after me to tell him other stories but I told him, sure I was a storyteller but I only did one at a time. He then told me that he wrote stories and that he was going to tell me one of them if I wanted. I told him ,yes, and he went to get a copybook with several short stories. They had not been published yet. It didn't matter for getting published is always hard to do. My stories are only for people who care about stories enough to really want to listen to them like stories before going to bed. Besides, I'm a doll. Publishers would not want to publish me since I have nothing in writing. I get stories from others and then I tell them. If you're a storyteller you tell the stories and you don't necessarily read them out of a book. You tell them. You know what I mean.

Michael called me "ma chouette. the feminine of mon chou, I suppose. My cabbage! It sounds better in French. Here is what Michael told me. It's a story of a doll who escapes from the doll house. The doll was a Raggedy Ann cloth doll. Yes, Raggedy Anns are entirely made of cloth. No plastic, no enamel, no glass, no rubber, nothing of the sort, just cloth. It was designed that way. I know I was there.

I found out that it was a man from somewhere in Indiana who first thought of a rag doll with hair made out of red yarn, button eyes, a triangular stamped nose, and someone at one time or another stamped the doll's chest with a red heart. I don't know why they call it a "rag" doll for Raggedy Ann is not made out of rags.

She is definitely made of cloth.She's very pliable and very easy to handle and I beleive as a doll she's good handling for young children even babies. They can swing her around, toss her up in the air. drop her on the floor, even step on her and she will not scream nor will she get angry like many dolls would if handled roughly like that. I know of one doll who would slap you in the face if you did that to her. I won't give you her name for that would create an incident for me. I'm pretty docile and I don't like incidents especially a fight with another doll. It can be vicious, you know. Of course, you don't know anything about dolls fighting but believe me it exists. Crazy!

I was there when Johnny Gruelle discovered an old cloth doll in his mother's attic one day. I happened to be visiting old Mrs Gruelle' house that day. I was with Michael Guay, remember him? He was with a friend who knew the Gruelles and his name was Johnny Macallister. Well, the three of us went to pay a visit to the Gruelles and we somehow went to Mrs. Gruelle's house where Johnny Gruelle was staying with his wife, Myrtle, for the week. When we came in, old Mrs. Gruelle received us with smiles and bright eyes. I would say they were twinkling. Then we met her son, Johnny, who asked Michael, if he could take me in his hands and look at me. He seemed very interested in dolls, I suppose. He asked what was my name and Michael told him, Founie. "Founie?", he said, "What a strange name." "It may be but that's her name. It's a crazy kind of name but it's hers." I wished I could have told him that my name was not crazy but nice. It was my name and I liked it. It was altogether rare and unique, I thought. So please, please respect my name. It's mine and nobody else's; no other doll has that name. None, I tell you.

So Johnny Gruelle took me and started examining me. He noticed my sticker and shouted, "Why it's in French." His wife insisted that he tell her what it meant. "Wait a minute now. Le bonheur. yes happiness. It says to those who possess me I bring happiness. Can you imagine that? A doll, a rather cheap one probably from a flea market at that bringing happiness to a human being? Why I can't believe it." Everyone wanted to glance at my blouse and my sticker. I wanted to tell them all to get their paws off-a me. I wanted to say that I wasn't a cheap doll. Sure I was a flea market doll, but I was not a cheap one, no sirree, I was not cheap and I certainly was not a poor thing without character or meaning. I was a doll of circumstances, rich and meaningful circumstances. I had seen different people in various cities and countries and I had learned a lot. I might be poor in things and riches but rich in learning and judgement, I'll have you know. Only Myrtle was not unkind to me; she was a gentle person, it seemed to me. The old Mrs. Gruelle just stood there smiling like a odd fixture waiting her turn to speak.

Johnny Gruelle then told his wife, his mother and the three of us that he had found an old cloth doll in the attic and that he was going to build an entire character on this doll. A lost ragamuffin of a doll somehow abandoned in his mother's attic. He was going to write books about her, the doll. That he was going to call her "Rags" or something like that. His wife told him not to call her that for it would sound cheap and not very civil. "Give the doll a proper name, Johnny," said Myrtle. Later on, we found out that he had named his creation of a doll "Raggedy Ann."

Johmmy Gruelle wrote many stories about Raggedy Ann and later wrote about Raggedy Ann's brother, Raggedy Andy that he had created. Eventually the cloth doll that I had seen became so popular that it sold in the millions. So many parents made the Raggedy Ann doll their favorite gift for their child because they knew it would become the child's favorite toy. Always smiling, always gay, always easy to handle and always loved, the Raggedy Ann doll was world famous and to think I could have been like her. Millions could have been sold. Millions of Founies and her sticker could have been produced. However, I didn't want that and so did my owner, if I ever had an owner. I had many a responsible handler but no owner really. I don't know if people would have liked the name Founie anyways. Founie la poupée qui apporte le bonheur, a fortunate owner but an unfortunate circumstance of from hand to hand to hand and eventually into the marché aux puces/ the flea market. What a dump for some while a treasure trove for others. It's hilarious. It's sublime. It's crazy! That's what I say.

Then I heard of another cloth doll named Orphan Annie. Another redhead. Wow! I don't know what was the color of my hair, since I only had a semblance of hair, not real hair. A lick of plastic hair, that's all I had. I would have liked red hair.

That's so exciting and so desirable for a doll like me. I could have been on the world market like these two cloth dolls. Anyway, I remain a doll that brings happiness to whoever will one day possess me, me Foonie the plastic doll with a sticker, a sticker yellowed with the years. Yellow because no one

YOUNIE, THE FLEA MARKET DOLL

wanted me. No one wanted to keep me. It's sad when no one wants you. Would you want me? I'm Founie the looney one, the doll that seeks an unhappy one in order to bring her or him happiness. Happiness exists you know but you have to find it and you have to deserve happiness. It's not free. You have to give something for it. You have to give of yourself before you merit it. Some people only want to take and not give. Then that becomes a taking/take thing. Like an attic full of stuff that's often forgotten. You have to give and give and give in your lifetime, people. Giving is the key to happiness, my dear children. You are all my children. I have begotten you. How? Yes, you might ask me how? Through my imagination. I imagine things, you know. If I cannot be pregnant with a human child, then I imagine giving birth to one, to two, to three, to dozens and dozens, to thousands, to millions of them. Do you want me to continue? Then someone said, "Stop, do not continue this absurdity. It's another theater of the absurd." Alright, let us all be absurd in our thoughts and actions. "Then what?" asked someone else. "The whole world would turn absurd." "Isn't that what it already is?"" another one asked. I then said, Stop it! Stop it! are you all mad? Silence. The silence of people gone mad, I suppose. The entire evening was absurd and mad, I would say. Reasonableness was gone, it seemed. That's what happens when human reason seems to disappear. That's what I learned and that's what I say.

Well, enough of this babbling and speech making stuff. I know that I bore you with all of this, what I call stuff. Stuff can be very stuffy and stuffing. Like stuffing a turkey. The poor turkey is dead and they will put it in the oven and roast it so that people will eat it with the stuffing. It's a good thing I'm a doll and not a turkey. A poor flea market doll but a happy doll who learned so many things among people like you. Founie that's who I am.et j'apporte le bonheur à qui me possède.

I have one last thing to tell you and that's how did I get to the flea market near the Porte de Clignancourt in Paris. Well, pay attention folks and I will tell you. When I got back to Paris and Marianne my indulgent and faithful caregiver and confidant, I was told that Marianne was not feeling well. She had cancer of the brain or tumors that were evolving into cancer. Something like that. She never mentioned it to me or to anyone not even Antoine. Then her mother told Antoine that her daughter did not have long to live. I felt so very sad for both of them, sad and devastated for poor Marianne who had been so good to me. I certainly did not bring her happiness. She told me that she was happy just the same for she had touched base with so many old friends as well as new ones. She had wanted that and wanting to share me with people who would appreciate my gift as a doll. I asked her what that gift was. She told me that a doll whoever she is, is a gift to someone simply by her presence of loving and being loved. You see she understood that wanting/wanted was a gift of love and love became the very heart of the gift. Oh, good Lord, I was a gift, a gift of love. So many people do not accept that dolls can love as well as people do. It's a two-way street. So people, please understand that dolls can love too, at least as far as I'm concerned. Imagine not being able to love. That's not living and existing. Might as well be totally passive and neutral or...dead. That's not me, people, Not me....pas moi.

Well, when Marianne passed away and was buried in the Père Lachaise cemetery in Paris, I was given to Antoine who in turn gave me to a friend of his. But this friend had no need of me. Why he even wanted to get rid of my sticker but he could not get it off. He didn't believe in happiness. He told his brother that happiness was but a fantasy, a dream if not a nightmare. I totally did not believe him and his sad state of affairs. You see, he did drugs and he was forever in the not so la-la-land, a land of horrible dreams of unhappiness. So, I bounced from hand to hand to grasping hand of fate. Where would I end up, I kept asking myself. One day, I fell into the hands of a young gitl named Mirette whose parents were very very poor with nothing to call theit own. All that Mirette had was me, the doll that brought happiness. She clung to me with all her heart and soul. I could tell. However, the parents had to move out of town and they had to get rid of stuff, whatever stuff they possessed which wasn't much. They even told Mirette she had to get rid of me, the cheap doll, they told her. Mirette refused as she persisted in clinging to me. Well, one night the parents stealthtily took me from their sleeping daughter and hid me in a barrel somewhere where they would retieve me the following day to sell me to a flea market holder of junk and things people wanted to get rid of. I was no longer wanted. Think of it, no longer wanted. And so that's what happened to me, the end and the beginning of my story. Believe me, life is like a spinning wheel(some call it a wheel of fortune), round and round we go and nobody knows where it will stop. Probably at death's door. Who knows. Do dolls die? I wonder. People die but they have an afterlife. I don't expect one. What I expect

YOUNIE, THE FLEA MARKET DOLL

is a doll receiver who wants and seeks happiness. Are you the one?

Norman Beaupré

YOUNIE, THE FLEA MARKET DOLL